THE
GOSPEL OF
MATTHEW:
DISPENSATIONALLY CONSIDERED

A GRACE EXPOSITIONAL COMMENTARY

Dr. David Alan Greene

GraceWord Publishing, LLC
www.gracewordpublishing.com
U.S.A.

GRACEWORD PUBLISHING

Contents

To B'nai Avraham — the children of Abraham

Now I say that
Jesus Christ
was a minister of the circumcision
for the truth of God,
to confirm the promises
made unto the fathers:

– The Apostle Paul

x

Acknowledgements

I would like to express a special thanks to Jon and Susan McMahon and Frances Greene for their continued encouragement. To Marcella Lloyd, who assisted with the preparation of this book, I offer my gratitude.

Introduction

This introduction will play a key role in understanding the Gospel of Matthew. The reader should
be familiar with the concept and application of
rightly dividing the Word of Truth. It is also known
as the dispensational approach to Scripture. To sum-
marize, God created the Bible by dividing it into ages
or dispensations. Each of these divisions were intended to lead towards His ultimate goal of restoring
His Creation.

Traditionally, the Bible has been divided into
seven ages or periods of time. Sometimes, these divisions are referred to as administrations in which God
chose to make Himself known. There is a progres-
sion in these administrations which leads to its conclusion. Jumping into the middle of a book or movie
series does not allow the reader to fully understand
or enjoy the series in full.

GraceWord Publishing has created the Grace
Expositional Bible Commentary. Each of the books

included in the series walks the reader through the biblical book verse-by-verse. As this is done, it applies a system or method of interpretation. For this reason, I recommend the reader be familiar with the simple concept of "rightly dividing" the Word of Truth. Paul instructed his student, Timothy, in 2 Timothy 2:15:

> **15 Study to shew thyself approved unto God, a workman that needeth not to be ashamed, <u>rightly dividing the word of truth.</u>**

To understand any portion of Scripture, it must be seen within it proper division. It is dangerous to take verses of Scripture out of its context. Doing so will increase the risk of missing the point entirely or misunderstanding to whom the text was intended.

Like the number of days that God took to create the earth, I believe there are seven periods of time or ages or dispensations that He will take to redeem His Creation. The Gospel of Matthew opens in the middle of the fifth dispensation which is the Age of Law. The Jews received the Law from Moses after God used him to lead His people out of Egypt. It was in the Wilderness that God created Israel to be a "peculiar" or special people — a holy nation separated from all the other nations. Israel has a purpose!

God told Moses to speak to Israel. Exodus 19:6:

6 And ye shall be unto me <u>a kingdom of priests</u>, and <u>an holy nation</u>. These are the words which thou shalt speak unto the children of Israel.

The word "holy" means "separated." This was God's ultimate purpose for Israel. They will play a key role in His restored Creation.

Mosaic Covenant

Through Moses, God offered the children of Abraham, Isaac, and Jacob a binding contract or covenant. It would contractually bind God and His people. In the verses that follow, notice the offer and the acceptance. The people bound themselves to this conditional agreement. Verses 7-8:

7 And Moses came and called for the elders of the people, and laid before their faces all these words which the LORD commanded him.

8 <u>And all the people answered together, and said, All that the LORD hath spoken we will do</u>. And Moses returned the words of the people unto the LORD.

This agreement or covenant remains in effect. This fact is important. Nothing has changed for the Jews since the day they voluntarily accepted the terms of this agreement. God has not voided this covenant.

This means that the Law continues in full effect throughout Jesus' earthly ministry and thereafter. Consider His words in the Sermon of the Mount. A multitude of Jews gathered to hear Him speak. Matthew 5:17-18:

> 17 **Think not that I am come to destroy the law, or the prophets: I am not come to destroy, but to fulfil.**
>
> 18 **For verily I say unto you, <u>Till heaven and earth pass, one jot or one tittle shall in no wise pass from the law</u>, <u>till</u> [until it] <u>all be fulfilled</u>.**

So, the Law will be fulfilled at the end of the restoration. Jesus Christ is the One Who fulfills the Law.

Even after His death and resurrection, those who followed his Gospel of the Kingdom remain bound to the Law. Much later, the Apostle James wrote to the children of Abraham as they await the return of their Messiah. Look how he addresses his letter which he sent to comfort and encourage these

Kingdom Believers. James 1:1:

> 1 **James, a servant of God and of the Lord Jesus Christ, <u>to the twelve tribes which are scattered abroad, greeting.</u>**

Knowing to whom James wrote this letter reveals something important. It becomes clear that the Law still remains in effect for the Jews who follow the Gospel of the Kingdom. James, who was one of the Twelve, wrote this in verse 2:10:

> 10 **For whosoever shall keep the whole law, and yet offend in one point, he is guilty of all.**

He is reminding them of their obligation according to the Mosaic Covenant. The entire Law was read aloud to those in the Wilderness as it is read to the congregation every year. Consider again their response. Exodus 19:8:

> 8 **And all the people answered together, and said, <u>All that the LORD hath spoken we will do.</u> And Moses returned the words of the people unto the LORD.**

Notice it is not "some" of what God said, but "all" that God said. The first five books of the Bible are called the "books of Moses." In the fifth book, Deuteronomy, there is a portion of the Mosaic Covenant which is referred to as the "blessings and curses." This makes it clear that the covenant is conditional. IF they obey and do what is right according to the covenant, THEN God will bless them. However, IF they break one point of the covenant, THEN God will curse or punish them. James reiterates this point in his letter to them. He reminds them of their commitment to this lasting covenant.

Since evidence speaks louder that opinion, here are two portions from Deuteronomy 28. The first refers to the blessings. Verses 1-2:

> 1 **And it shall come to pass, if thou shalt hearken diligently unto the voice of the LORD thy God, <u>to observe and to do all his commandments which I command thee this day</u>, that [then] the LORD thy God will set thee on high above all nations of the earth:**

> 2 **And all these blessings shall come on thee, and overtake thee, if thou shalt hearken unto the voice of the LORD thy God.**

The consequence of failing to keep the Law in its entirety results in curses. Verse 15:

> 15 But it shall come to pass, if thou wilt not hearken unto the voice of the LORD thy God, <u>to observe to do all his commandments and his statutes which I command thee this day;</u> <u>that</u> [then] <u>all these curses shall come upon thee, and overtake thee:</u>

It is important to notice that in both references, the word "all" plays a key part in the effect it will have upon the children of Abraham, Isaac, and Israel.

From Moses, King David, his son King Solomon, and all the Old Testament prophets, the Law of Moses was in effect. Nothing had changed when Jesus was born. The Apostle Paul explains that <u>Jesus was under the Law</u> and <u>His purpose was to redeem those who were under the Law</u>. Galatians 4:4-5:

> 4 But when the fulness of the time was come, God sent forth his Son, made of a woman, <u>made under the law,</u> 5 <u>To redeem them that were under the law,</u> that we [they] might receive the adoption of sons.

There are two other covenants in the Old Testament that will have an impact on the people in the Gospel of Matthew. In addition to the Mosaic Covenant, other covenants were made with Abraham and King David. The Jews were taught well and they knew their Scripture. It gave them hope for the future because they trusted that God would fulfill His promises. Both of these are unconditional. This means that God will fulfill these covenants regardless of Israel's actions. Here, they are summarized:

Abrahamic Covenant:

The following is found in Genesis 12:1-3:

1 **Now the LORD had said unto Abram, Get thee out of thy country, and from thy kindred, and from thy father's house, unto a land that I will shew thee:**

2 **And I will make of thee a great nation, and I will bless thee, and make thy name great; and thou shalt be a blessing:**

3 **And I will bless them that bless thee, and curse him that curseth thee: and in thee shall all families of the earth be blessed.**

Davidic Covenant:

God told the prophet Nathan to deliver this message to King David. 2 Samuel 7:12-13:

> 12 **And when thy days be fulfilled, and thou shalt sleep with thy fathers, <u>I will set up thy seed after thee</u>, which shall proceed out of thy bowels, <u>and I will establish his kingdom.</u>**
>
> 13 **He shall build an house for my name, and <u>I will stablish the throne of his kingdom for ever.</u>**

The Seed or Son of David is Jesus Christ. Verses 14-16:

> 14 **I will be his father, and he shall be my son. If he commit iniquity, I will chasten him with the rod of men, and with the stripes of the children of men: 15 But my mercy shall not depart away from him, as I took it from Saul, whom I put away before thee.**
>
> 16 **And thine house and thy kingdom shall be established for ever before thee: thy throne shall be established for**

ever.

I believe knowing these facts adds a deeper understanding of the Word of Truth. For the more advanced student, you may wish to consider reading *Letters To Theophilus: Are You Ready For The End Times?* and *The Glorious Destiny of Israel: The Fulfillment of God's Promises and Prophecies to Israel.* These two books present "two sides of the same coin" from the perspective of both the non-Jew and Jew respectively. Others may enjoy reading an overall summary of the Bible found in *The Hidden Gospel.* It highlights key events in the Bible and explains in simple terms how it all comes together in the end.

It is my hope that more people will learn, understand, and enjoy their Bible.

1

About the Apostle Matthew

We begin in the land of Israel which is under the control of the Roman Empire. Rome had established Herod the Great as their king. He ruled from 37 B.C. to 4 A.D. He was the one who ordered the killing of infants in response to the arrival of the Magi at the birth of the Christ. There were also scribes and priests who administered the religious affairs of the Jews. The Temple was in full operation with its priesthood overseeing the daily sacrifices offered for the sins of the people.

Matthew was not liked by the people. He was a Jew who had been appointed to collect taxes or tribute on Rome's behalf. He is also known by his Hebrew name of Levi. Jesus' calling of Matthew as a disciple is recorded in all three of the synoptic gospels. These first three gospels present an historical record of Jesus' life and ministry. They share a similarity in their content and ordering of events. Here is what can be gleaned concerning the calling of Matthew:

Matthew 9:9–13:

> 9 And as Jesus passed forth from thence, he saw a man, named Matthew, sitting at the receipt of custom: and he saith unto him, Follow me. And he arose, and followed him.

> 10 And it came to pass, as Jesus sat at meat [a meal] in the house, behold, many publicans and sinners came and sat down with him and his disciples. 11 And when the Pharisees saw it, they said unto his disciples, Why eateth your Master with publicans and sinners?

> 12 But when Jesus heard that, he said unto them, They that be whole need not a physician, but they that are sick. 13 But go ye and learn what that meaneth, I will have mercy, and not sacrifice: for I am not come to call the righteous, but sinners to repentance.

Mark 2:13–17:

13 And he went forth again by the sea side; and all the multitude resorted unto him, and he taught them. 14 And as he passed by, he saw Levi the son of Alphaeus sitting at the receipt of custom, and said unto him, Follow me. And he arose and followed him.

15 And it came to pass, that, as Jesus sat at meat in his house, many publicans and sinners sat also together with Jesus and his disciples: for there were many, and they followed him.

16 And when the scribes and Pharisees saw him eat with publicans and sinners, they said unto his disciples, How is it that he eateth and drinketh with publicans and sinners?

17 When Jesus heard it, he saith unto them, They that are whole have no need of the physician, but they that are sick: I came not to call the righteous, but sinners to repentance.

Luke 5:27–32:

27 And after these things he went forth,

and saw a publican, named Levi, sitting at the receipt of custom: and he said unto him, Follow me. 28 And he left all, rose up, and followed him.

29 And Levi made him a great feast in his own house: and there was a great company of publicans and of others that sat down with them. 30 But their scribes and Pharisees murmured against his disciples, saying, Why do ye eat and drink with publicans and sinners?

31 And Jesus answering said unto them, They that are whole need not a physician; but they that are sick. 32 I came not to call the righteous, but sinners to repentance.

We will see how the other disciples were chosen by Jesus within Matthew's narrative. Matthew accepted Jesus. His desire to learn more about this man Jesus drew him to follow after Him.

2

Matthew 1

In royal courts, throughout history, the heredity of the monarchy is important. It records the line of succession and eligibility to the throne. The following proves that Matthew is the continuation of the Old Testament. He begins with establishing the line of succession to David's throne at the beginning of his gospel. Notice that it includes two important men of whom Jesus is a direct descendent: Abraham and King David. His connection to the covenants will become apparent as we continue. Matthew 1:1:

> 1 **The book of the generation of <u>Jesus Christ, the son of David, the son of Abraham.</u>**

Matthew begins with Abraham and follows His geneaology up to Joseph at His birth. Verses 2-16:

2 Abraham begat Isaac; and Isaac begat Jacob; and Jacob begat Judas and his brethren; 3 And Judas begat Phares and Zara of Thamar; and Phares begat Esrom; and Esrom begat Aram; 4 And Aram begat Aminadab; and Aminadab begat Naasson; and Naasson begat Salmon; 5 And Salmon begat Boaz of Rachab; and Boaz begat Obed of Ruth; and Obed begat Jesse;

6 And Jesse begat David the king; and David the king begat Solomon of her that had been the wife of Urias; 7 And Solomon begat Roboam; and Roboam begat Abia; and Abia begat Asa; 8 And Asa begat Josaphat; and Josaphat begat Joram; and Joram begat Ozias; 9 And Ozias begat Joatham; and Joatham begat Achaz; and Achaz begat Ezekias; 10 And Ezekias begat Manasses; and Manasses begat Amon; and Amon begat Josias; 11 And Josias begat Jechonias and his brethren, about the time they were carried away to Babylon:

12 And after they were brought to Babylon, Jechonias begat Salathiel; and Salathiel begat Zorobabel;

13 And Zorobabel begat Abiud; and Abiud begat Eliakim; and Eliakim begat Azor; **14** And Azor begat Sadoc; and Sadoc begat Achim; and Achim begat Eliud; **15** And Eliud begat Eleazar; and Eleazar begat Matthan; and Matthan begat Jacob;

16 And Jacob begat Joseph the husband of Mary, of whom was born Jesus, who is called Christ.

The order and structure of God's work is never haphazard or chaotic. It is always in order and often numerically balanced. Matthew shows us a majestic beauty in its structure that is worthy of admiration. Verse 17:

17 So all the generations from Abraham to David are fourteen generations; and from David until the carrying away into Babylon are fourteen generations; and from the carrying away into Babylon unto Christ are fourteen generations.

The Gospel of Matthew provides the details concerning the birth of the Savior which are often read aloud in Christmas services. Verses 18-21:

18 Now the birth of Jesus Christ was on this wise [way]: When as his mother Mary was espoused to Joseph, before they came together, she was found with child of the Holy Ghost. **19** Then Joseph her husband, being a just man, and not willing to make her a public example, was minded to put her away privily.

20 But while he thought on these things, behold, the angel of the Lord appeared unto him in a dream, saying, Joseph, thou son of David, fear not to take unto thee Mary thy wife: for that which is conceived in her is of the Holy Ghost.

21 And she shall bring forth a son, and thou shalt call his name JESUS: <u>for he shall save his people</u> from their sins.

The name Jesus in Hebrew is Yeshua and in English is Joshua. It means "God is deliverance" or "God is salvation."

We must not forget the prophetic nature of His miraculous birth. The Hebrew prophets told the people what would happen. In turn, they earnestly looked forward with anticipation for these promises to be fulfilled. Now, it was happening before their eyes! (See Isaiah 7:14.)Verses 22-25:

> 22 Now all this was done, that it might be fulfilled which was spoken of the Lord by the prophet, saying, 23 Behold, a virgin shall be with child, and shall bring forth a son, and they shall call his name Emmanuel, which being interpreted is, God with us.
>
> 24 Then Joseph being raised from sleep did as the angel of the Lord had bidden him, and took unto him his wife: 25 And knew her not till she had brought forth her firstborn son: and he called his name JESUS.

3

Matthew 2

All this happened while Herod the Great was ruling. The birth of the Savior was not met with joy by all. For the powers, principalities, and rulers of darkness were filled with anger. The opposition now knew that the light had come and they would seek every opportunity to extinguish that light. Matthew 2:1-3:

> 1 **Now when Jesus was born in Bethlehem of Judaea in the days of Herod the king, behold, there came wise men from the east to Jerusalem, 2 Saying, <u>Where is he that is born King of the Jews?</u> for we have seen his star in the east, and are come to worship him. 3 When Herod the king had heard these things, he was troubled, and all Jerusalem with him.**

Those in power rarely like change especially if it threatens the status quo. Based upon what Herod learned, it is understandable that he would go to great lengths to prevent this change from happening. Verses 4-11:

> 4 And when he had gathered all the chief priests and scribes of the people together, he demanded of them where Christ should be born. 5 And they said unto him, In Bethlehem of Judaea: for thus it is written by the prophet,

> 6 And thou Bethlehem, in the land of Juda, art not the least among the princes of Juda: for out of thee shall come a Governor, that shall rule my people Israel.

> 7 Then Herod, when he had privily called the wise men, enquired of them diligently what time the star appeared. 8 And he sent them to Bethlehem, and said, Go and search diligently for the young child; and when ye have found him, bring me word again, that I may come and worship him also.

> 9 When they had heard the king, they

departed; and, lo, the star, which they saw in the east, went before them, till it came and stood over where the young child was. 10 When they saw the star, they rejoiced with exceeding great joy.

11 And when they were come into the house, they saw the young child with Mary his mother, and fell down, and worshipped him: and when they had opened their treasures, they presented unto him gifts; gold, and frankincense, and myrrh.

This was a time of rejoicing for God had fulfilled His promise to provide Israel with their Messiah Who would save them. However, the adversary did not want this to happen.

Joseph and Mary, the mother of Jesus, were warned of the danger to the Child. Verses 12-15:

12 And being warned of God in a dream that they should not return to Herod, they departed into their own country another way.

13 And when they were departed, be-

hold, the angel of the Lord appeareth to Joseph in a dream, saying, Arise, and take the young child and his mother, and flee into Egypt, and be thou there until I bring thee word: for Herod will seek the young child to destroy him.

14 When he arose, he took the young child and his mother by night, and departed into Egypt: 15 And was there until the death of Herod: that it might be fulfilled which was spoken of the Lord by the prophet, saying, Out of Egypt have I called my son.

Similar to the calling of the children of Abraham out of Egypt, God would also call His Son out of Egypt. (See Hosea 11:1.)

King Herod's solution to this problem was to kill all the children two years of age and younger. Verses 16-18:

16 Then Herod, when he saw that he was mocked of the wise men, was exceeding wroth [angry], and sent forth, and slew all the children that were in Bethlehem, and in all the coasts thereof, from two years old and under, according to the

time which he had diligently enquired of the wise men.

17 Then was fulfilled that which was spoken by Jeremiah the prophet, saying, 18 In Rama was there a voice heard, lamentation, and weeping, and great mourning, Rachel weeping for her children, and would not be comforted, because they are not.

Joseph was told to wait until he received news of Herod's death. We can estimate that Jesus was about four years old at the time. Returning, they found that Herod's son Archelaus had replaced him. So they headed to Galilee and settled in Nazareth. Verses 19-23:

19 But when Herod was dead, behold, an angel of the Lord appeareth in a dream to Joseph in Egypt, 20 Saying, Arise, and take the young child and his mother, and go into the land of Israel: for they are dead which sought the young child's life.

21 And he arose, and took the young child and his mother, and came into the land of Israel. 22 But when he heard that

Archelaus did reign in Judaea in the room of his father Herod, he was afraid to go thither: notwithstanding, being warned of God in a dream, he turned aside into the parts of Galilee:

23 And he came and dwelt in a city called Nazareth: that it might be fulfilled which was spoken by the prophets, He shall be called a Nazarene.

4

Matthew 3

We are not given much information about Jesus' youth. There is one story in the Gospel of Luke about Jesus when He was twelve years old. You can read that story in Luke 2:40-52. Matthew chose to move to the arrival of John the Baptist who was foretold by both the prophets Isaiah and Malachi. (See Isa. 40:3 and Mal. 3:1.) John the Baptist was the herald who proclaims the arrival of the Messiah. (See Isaiah 40:3.) Matthew 3:1-3:

> 1 **In those days came John the Baptist, preaching in the wilderness of Judaea, 2 And saying, <u>Repent ye: for the kingdom of heaven is at hand.</u>**
>
> 3 **For this is he that was spoken of by the prophet Esaias, saying, The voice of one crying in the wilderness, Prepare ye the**

way of the Lord, make his paths
straight.

Here, we have a description of John. His ministry was to proclaim the coming of the Messiah and
call the Jews to repent and be baptized. Verses 4-6:

> 4 **And the same John had his raiment of
> camel's hair, and a leathern girdle about
> his loins; and his meat was locusts and
> wild honey.**

> 5 **Then went out to him Jerusalem, and
> all Judaea, and all the region round
> about Jordan, 6 And were baptized of
> [by] him in Jordan, confessing their
> sins.**

We are not long into the gospel when we are
introduced to the opposition that will follow the
Messiah throughout His ministry. They are the religious leaders to whom Jesus would pose a threat.
The Pharisees and Sadducees are similar but the latter do not believe in a resurrection. Verses 7-8:

> 7 **But when he saw many of the Phari-
> sees and Sadducees come to his bap-
> tism, he said unto them, O generation of
> vipers, who hath warned you to flee**

18

from the wrath to come?

8 **Bring forth therefore fruits meet [acceptable] for repentance:**

This will become a theme throughout the New Testament. For salvation, the Jews will be required to provide evidence of their faith. Without works as proof, they are left with only empty platitudes. Simply being descendants of Abraham does not secure their future. Jesus said that God could make stones into children of Abraham. Verse 9:

9 **And think not to say within yourselves, We have Abraham to our father: for I say unto you, that God is able of these stones to raise up children unto Abraham.**

The following is the first direct warning to the religious leaders of the coming judgment. Verse 10:

10 **And now also the axe is laid unto the root of the trees: therefore every tree which bringeth not forth good fruit is hewn down, and cast into the fire.**

John makes his role in this clear. He is only there to tell them about the coming Messiah. The One Who will bring both salvation and the judgment of God is the Messiah. Verses 11-12:

> 11 I [John] indeed baptize you with water unto repentance: but he that cometh after me is mightier than I, whose shoes I am not worthy to bear: he shall baptize you with the Holy Ghost, and with fire:

> 12 Whose fan is in his hand, and he will throughly purge his floor, and gather his wheat into the garner [granary]; but he will burn up the chaff with unquenchable fire.

We are told that the Messiah has arrived and He has come to be baptized by John. Notice John's reaction. Jesus certainly does not need to repent. Matthew explains. Verses 13-15:

> 13 Then cometh Jesus from Galilee to Jordan unto John, to be baptized of [by] him. 14 But John forbad him, saying, I have need to be baptized of thee, and comest thou to me?

> 15 And Jesus answering said unto him, Suffer [Allow] it to be so now: for thus it becometh us to fulfil all righteous-

ness. Then he suffered [allowed] him.

Righteousness for the Jews begins with the sign of baptism which is a symbolic or ritual cleansing.

God publicly acknowledges His approval of His Son following this baptism. Verses 16-17:

> 16 **And Jesus, when he was baptized, went up straightway out of the water: and, lo, the heavens were opened unto him, and he saw the Spirit of God descending like a dove, and lighting upon him:**
>
> 17 **And lo a voice from heaven, saying, <u>This is my beloved Son, in whom I am well pleased</u>.**

5

Matthew 4

The use of certain numbers play an important part in Jewish history. Some theologians believe that it was possible for the children of Israel to traverse the Wilderness from Egypt to the Promised Land in forty days. If they walked at 3 miles per hour for six hours and they did this only six days a week, then it was possible. Unfortunately, <u>they failed their test through lack of faith</u> and it became a forty-year ordeal.

Before Jesus could begin His earthly ministry, He too, like Israel, must be tested. Matthew 4:1-2:

> 1 **Then was Jesus led up of the Spirit into the wilderness to be tempted of the devil. 2 And when he had fasted forty days and forty nights, he was afterward an hungred.**

At His weakest physical point, Satan begins his temptations with three tests. Everyone is tested with temptation, but notice how Jesus uses the Word of God to refute Satan. Verses 3-11:

> 3 And when the tempter came to him, he said, If thou be the Son of God, [then] command that these stones be made bread. 4 But he answered and said, <u>It is written</u>, Man shall not live by bread alone, but by every word that proceedeth out of the mouth of God.

> 5 Then the devil taketh him up into the holy city, and setteth him on a pinnacle of the temple, 6 And saith unto him, If thou be the Son of God, [then] cast thyself down: for it is written, He shall give his angels charge concerning thee: and in their hands they shall bear thee up, lest at any time thou dash thy foot against a stone. 7 Jesus said unto him, <u>It is written</u> again, Thou shalt not tempt the Lord thy God.

> 8 Again, the devil taketh him up into an exceeding high mountain, and sheweth him all the kingdoms of the world, and the glory of them; 9 And saith unto him,

All these things will I give thee, if thou wilt fall down and worship me. 10 **Then saith Jesus unto him, Get thee hence, Satan: for <u>it is written</u>, Thou shalt worship the Lord thy God, and him only shalt thou serve.**

11 **Then the devil leaveth him, and, behold, angels came and ministered unto him.**

The Word of God is powerful as we see later in the book of Hebrews. Hebrews 4:12:

12 **For <u>the word of God</u> is quick, and powerful, and sharper than any two-edged sword, piercing even to the dividing asunder of soul and spirit, and of the joints and marrow, and is a discerner of the thoughts and intents of the heart.**

Knowing and understanding the Bible can be a valuable tool available for the believer's defense.

With His period of testing successfully completed, Jesus will begin His earthly ministry. Matthew 4:12-16:

12 Now when Jesus had heard that John was cast into prison, he departed into Galilee; **13** And leaving Nazareth, he came and dwelt in Capernaum, which is upon the sea coast, in the borders of Zabulon and Nephthalim:

14 That it might be fulfilled which was spoken by Esaias the prophet, saying, **15** The land of Zabulon, and the land of Nephthalim, by the way of the sea, beyond Jordan, Galilee of the Gentiles;

16 The people which sat in darkness saw great light; and to them which sat in the region and shadow of death light is sprung up.

This great light was to the Jews who sat in darkness which was their ignorance of God's plan for redemption. This light was Jesus. He would continually make reference to this throughout His ministry. His message was simple. The word "repent" is best understood when compared to the military marching command, "About face." It means "to turn around and head in the opposite direction." Verse 17:

17 From that time Jesus began to preach, and to say, Repent: for the kingdom of

heaven is at hand.

He begins to choose His disciples which is another name for the students He will teach. The first are two brothers: Peter and Andrew. Verses 18-20:

> 18 **And Jesus, walking by the sea of Galilee, saw two brethren, Simon called Peter, and Andrew his brother, casting a net into the sea: for they were fishers.**
>
> 19 **And he saith unto them, Follow me, and I will make you fishers of men.** 20 **And they straightway left their nets, and followed him.**

Jesus continues recruiting His disciples as He travels to meet the people. Verses 21-22:

> 21 **And going on from thence, he saw other two brethren, James the son of Zebedee, and John his brother, in a ship with Zebedee their father, mending their nets; and he called them.**
>
> 22 **And they immediately left the ship and their father, and followed him.**

The Sea of Galilee is located in the northern part of

Israel near Lebanon and Syria. Jesus traveled throughout the region preaching <u>the Gospel of the Kingdom</u>. Verse 23:

> **23 And Jesus went about all Galilee, teaching in their synagogues, and <u>preaching the gospel of the kingdom,</u> and healing all manner of sickness and all manner of disease among the people.**

The role of the Messiah has three offices. These are: prophet, priest, and king. At present, He is exercising His office as prophet. Following His resurrection, we learn that Jesus Christ will officiate as Israel's high priest of the order to Melchizedek in the heavenly tabernacle. (See Hebrews 7.) Later, in Revelation, Jesus will return as Israel's King to destroy their enemies and save His people. A prophet is someone who must be authenticated by miracles, signs, and wonders. These are proof that a prophet is certified by God. News of Jesus' acts of healing spread throughout the region. Verses 24-25:

> **24 And his fame went throughout all Syria: and they brought unto him all sick people that were taken with divers diseases and torments, and those which were possessed with devils, and those which were lunatick, and those that had**

the palsy; and he healed them.

25 And there followed him great multi-tudes of people from Galilee, and from Decapolis, and from Jerusalem, and from Judaea, and from beyond Jordan.

I would like to clarify something for the reader. In the verses above and those that follow, the words "the gospel of the kingdom" appear. This is a specific gospel message. Christ came to proclaim to Israel the good news of David's Kingdom in fulfillment of the promises. Paul explains to the Gentiles the purpose of Jesus' earthly ministry. Romans 15:8:

8 Now I say that <u>Jesus Christ was a min-ister of the circumcision [Israel] for the truth of God, to confirm the promises made unto the fathers:</u>

The "circumcision" are the children of Abraham. But, who are the fathers? Peter answers this in his speech at Pentecost. He speaks of the Messiah being from the brethren Who will confirm the covenant God made with "the fathers." He is the promised Seed of Abraham. Acts 3:22-25:

22 For Moses truly said unto <u>the fathers,</u> A prophet shall the Lord your God raise

up unto you of your brethren, like unto me [Moses]; him shall ye hear in all things whatsoever he shall say unto you.

23 And it shall come to pass, that every soul, which will not hear that prophet, shall be destroyed from among the people.

24 Yea, and all the prophets from Samuel and those that follow after, as many as have spoken, have likewise foretold of these days.

25 Ye are the children of the prophets, and of the covenant which God made with our fathers, saying unto Abraham, And in thy seed shall all the kindreds of the earth be blessed.

Soon, while visiting His hometown synagogue, Jesus will make a proclamation to the Jews concerning His mission.

6

Matthew 5

There is an event that followed Jesus' testing in the wilderness that was not included in Matthew's narrative. It provides an important insight into Jesus' mission. Luke 4:13-21:

> 13 And when the devil had ended all the temptation, he departed from him for a season. 14 And Jesus returned in the power of the Spirit into Galilee: and there went out a fame of him through all the region round about. 15 And he taught in their synagogues, being glorified of [by] all.

> 16 And he came to Nazareth, where he had been brought up: and, as his custom was, he went into the synagogue on the sabbath day, and stood up for to read.

17 And there was delivered unto him the book of the prophet Esaias. And when he had opened the book, he found the place where it was written, 18 <u>The Spirit of the Lord is upon me, because he hath anointed me to preach the gospel to the poor; he hath sent me to heal the brokenhearted, to preach deliverance to the captives, and recovering of sight to the blind, to set at liberty them that are bruised, 19 To preach the acceptable year of the Lord.</u>

20 And he closed the book, and he gave it again to the minister, and sat down. And the eyes of all them that were in the synagogue were fastened on him. 21 And he began to say unto them, <u>This day is this scripture fulfilled in your ears.</u>

One might think that all eyes were on Him because He was the local boy returned to Nazareth. However, He stopped in the middle of a verse and then sat down. The Jews knew this.

The word "and" sometimes denotes a lapse in time. The following sentence provides an example. She was born in London and died in Boston. There is clearly a span of time separated by the conjunction "and." Such is the case with this prophecy that He read aloud before the congregation. Isaiah 61:2

> 2 **To proclaim the acceptable year of the LORD, . . .**

This portion He had fulfilled. However, the remainder of the same verse will be fulfilled in the future.

> 2 **. . . and the day of vengeance of our God; to comfort all that mourn;**

This day of vengeance or punishment refers to the coming Tribulation.

Eager to see the miracles, a large mass of people followed Him. They were curious to learn more about Him and what He was teaching. The following is referred to as the Sermon on the Mount. There is a place in northern Israel called the Mount of the Beatitudes. It has a view overlooking the Sea of Galilee. Many believe that it was here that Jesus preached the following sermon. Matthew 5:1-12:

> 1 **And seeing the multitudes, he went up into a mountain: and when he was set, His disciples came unto him: 2 And he opened his mouth, and taught them,**

saying, 3 Blessed are the poor in spirit: for theirs is the kingdom of heaven.

4 Blessed are they that mourn: for they shall be comforted.

5 Blessed are the meek: for they shall inherit the earth.

6 Blessed are they which do hunger and thirst after righteousness: for they shall be filled.

7 Blessed are the merciful: for they shall obtain mercy.

8 Blessed are the pure in heart: for they shall see God.

9 Blessed are the peacemakers: for they shall be called the children of God.

10 Blessed are they which are persecuted for righteousness' sake: for theirs is the kingdom of heaven.

11 Blessed are ye, when men shall revile you, and persecute you, and shall say all

manner of evil against you falsely, for my sake.

12 Rejoice, and be exceeding glad: for great is your reward in heaven: for so persecuted they the prophets which were before you.

Jesus wanted them to rejoice and repent from the ways of their ancestors who persecuted the prophets.

He continues with His sermon. Verses 13-16:

13 Ye are the salt of the earth: but if the salt have lost his savour, wherewith shall it be salted? it is thenceforth good for nothing, but to be cast out, and to be trodden under foot of men.

14 Ye are the light of the world. A city that is set on an hill cannot be hid. 15 Neither do men light a candle, and put it under a bushel, but on a candlestick; and it giveth light unto all that are in the house.

16 Let your light so shine before men, that they may see your good works, and glorify your Father which is in heaven.

As previously mentioned, the requirements of the Law will not be diminished. Jesus confirms this will not change. The Mosaic Covenant was conditional. Depending on their compliance, it would result in either blessings or curses; life or death. For a solution, God sent His Son to fulfill the requirements of the Law on their behalf. Verses 17-20:

> 17 **Think not that I am come to destroy the law, or the prophets: I am not come to destroy, but to fulfil. 18 For verily I say unto you, Till heaven and earth pass, one jot or one tittle shall in no wise pass from the law, till all be fulfilled.**

> 19 **Whosoever therefore shall break one of these least commandments, and shall teach men so, he shall be called the least in the kingdom of heaven: but whosoever shall do and teach them, the same shall be called great in the kingdom of heaven.**

> 20 **For I say unto you, That except your righteousness shall exceed the righteousness of the scribes and Pharisees, ye shall in no case [way] enter into the kingdom of heaven.**

In the following portion of the sermon, Christ takes it beyond the letter of the Law to the Spirit of the Law. Verses 21-22:

21 **Ye have heard that it was said by them of old time, Thou shalt not kill; and whosoever shall kill shall be in danger of the judgment:**

22 **But I say unto you, That whosoever is angry with his brother without a cause shall be in danger of the judgment: and whosoever shall say to his brother, Raca, shall be in danger of the council: but whosoever shall say, Thou fool, shall be in danger of hell fire.**

Bringing tithes and offerings is a form of communion with God. To do this the worshipper must be in the right frame of mind. Verses 23-26:

23 **Therefore if thou bring thy gift to the altar, and there rememberest that thy brother hath ought [something] against thee; 24 Leave there thy gift before the altar, and go thy way; first be reconciled to thy brother, and then come and offer thy gift.**

25 Agree with thine adversary quickly, whiles thou art in the way with him; lest at any time the adversary deliver thee to the judge, and the judge deliver thee to the officer, and thou be cast into prison.

26 Verily I say unto thee, Thou shalt by no means come out thence, till thou hast paid the uttermost farthing.

Their relationship with God has much to do with their relationship with their neighbors. This theme which we could call the Law of Love is maintained throughout this gospel. Later, we will read this in Matthew 22:37-40:

37 Jesus said unto him, Thou shalt love the Lord thy God with all thy heart, and with all thy soul, and with all thy mind. **38** This is the first and great commandment.

39 And the second is like unto it, Thou shalt love thy neighbour as thyself. **40** On these two commandments hang all the law and the prophets.

He continues with going beyond the letter of the Law to the Spirit of the Law. Starting with what they have been taught He takes it to God's intent or purpose of the Law as expressed above. Now, we return to Matthew 5:27-44:

27 Ye have heard that it was said by them of old time, Thou shalt not commit adultery: 28 But I say unto you, That whosoever looketh on a woman to lust after her hath committed adultery with her already in his heart.

29 And if thy right eye offend thee, pluck it out, and cast it from thee: for it is profitable for thee that one of thy members should perish, and not that thy whole body should be cast into hell.

30 And if thy right hand offend thee, cut it off, and cast it from thee: for it is profitable for thee that one of thy members should perish, and not that thy whole body should be cast into hell.

31 It hath been said, Whosoever shall put away his wife, let him give her a writing of divorcement: 32 But I say unto you, That whosoever shall put away his wife, saving [except] for the cause of fornication, causeth her to commit adul-

tery: and whosoever shall marry her that is divorced committeth adultery.

33 Again, ye have heard that it hath been said by them of old time, Thou shalt not forswear thyself, but shalt perform unto the Lord thine oaths: 34 But I say unto you, Swear not at all; neither by heaven; for it is God's throne: 35 Nor by the earth; for it is his footstool: neither by Jerusalem; for it is the city of the great King. 36 Neither shalt thou swear by thy head, because thou canst not make one hair white or black. 37 But let your communication be, Yea, yea; Nay, nay: for whatsoever is more than these cometh of evil.

38 Ye have heard that it hath been said, An eye for an eye, and a tooth for a tooth: 39 But I say unto you, That ye resist not evil: but whosoever shall smite thee on thy right cheek, turn to him the other also.

40 And if any man will sue thee at the law, and take away thy coat, let him have thy cloke also. 41 And whosoever shall compel thee to go a mile, go with

him twain [two]. 42 Give to him that asketh thee, and from him that would borrow of thee turn not thou away.

43 Ye have heard that it hath been said, Thou shalt love thy neighbour, and hate thine enemy. 44 But I say unto you, Love your enemies, bless them that curse you, do good to them that hate you, and pray for them which despitefully use you, and persecute you;

All the above is to achieve one outcome. The children of Abraham are children of their heavenly Father. As such, they are expected to live accordingly among all people. Verses 45-48:

45 That ye may be the children of your Father which is in heaven: for he maketh his sun to rise on the evil and on the good, and sendeth rain on the just and on the unjust.

46 For if ye love them which love you, what reward have ye? do not even the publicans the same? 47 And if ye salute [greet] your brethren only, what do ye more than others? do not even the publicans [do] so?

48 Be ye therefore perfect, even [that is to say] as your Father which is in heaven is perfect.

7

Matthew 6

How Israel is to comply with the Law goes beyond mere empty actions. They must be heart-felt and genuine. Jesus continues with His teaching. The people had never heard anything like this before because it exceeded just compliance. While the teachers of the Law expounded on the mechanical means of fulfilling their obligations to the Law, Jesus was teaching a change of heart. Many of the religious leaders demonstrated their piousness by showing their acts of obedience. This was not what God desired. Matthew 6:1-8:

> **1 Take heed that ye do not your alms before men, to be seen of them: otherwise ye have no reward of your Father which is in heaven. 2 Therefore when thou doest thine alms, do not sound a trumpet before thee, as the hypocrites do in**

the synagogues and in the streets, that they may have glory of men. Verily I say unto you, They have their reward.

3 But when thou doest alms, let not thy left hand know what thy right hand doeth: 4 That thine alms may be in secret: and thy Father which seeth in secret himself shall reward thee openly.

5 And when thou prayest, thou shalt not be as the hypocrites are: for they love to pray standing in the synagogues and in the corners of the streets, that they may be seen of men. Verily I say unto you, They have their reward.

6 But thou, when thou prayest, enter into thy closet, and when thou hast shut thy door, pray to thy Father which is in secret; and thy Father which seeth in secret shall reward thee openly.

7 But when ye pray, use not vain repetitions, as the heathen do: for they think that they shall be heard for their much speaking. 8 Be not ye therefore like unto them: for your Father knoweth what things ye have need of, before ye ask

him.

Jesus provided the believers of the Gospel of the Kingdom with a model prayer they can follow. It is important that I point out that this model prayer applies to Kingdom Believers. It does not apply to Grace Believers or non-believers. Each has a unique relationship with God. As their model, each Kingdom Believer can fashion their own prayer by including the following components. Verses 9-10:

> 9 **After this manner therefore pray ye: Our Father which art in heaven, Hallowed be thy name. 10 Thy kingdom come. Thy will be done in earth, as it is in heaven.**

It will help believers to put God in the proper perspective by seeing Him as the all-powerful God. Asking for needs to be met acknowledges Him as the Giver of all good gifts. Verse 11:

> 11 **Give us this day our daily bread.**

As in the Wilderness, God provided Israel with manna on a "daily" basis to meet their "daily" need.

Concerning forgiveness, notice the comparison being made. Forgiveness will be granted in the same manner in which it is shown to others. Verse 12:

**12 And forgive us our debts, <u>as we for-
give our debtors.</u>**

The above cannot apply to those who are forgiven by grace through faith. (See Ephesians 2:8-9.) <u>Israel is required to keep the Law and to show continued proof of their faith.</u> How they forgive the trespasses of others affects how God responds to their request for forgiveness.

The prayer is closed with requests for direction and protection from evil; followed by an acknowledgement of God's eternal power and glory. Verse 13:

**13 And lead us not into temptation, but
deliver us from evil: For thine is the
kingdom, and the power, and the glory,
for ever. Amen.**

Those saved by the Gospel of Grace receive their salvation immediately and all sins (past, present, and future) are forgiven. Those saved by the Gospel of the Kingdom have certain conditions that must be met in order to obtain their salvation. Again, with them, their sins are forgiven in the same manner in which they forgive others. Verses 14-15:

14 For if ye forgive men their trespasses, your heavenly Father will also forgive you: 15 But if ye forgive not men their trespasses, neither will your Father forgive your trespasses.

We are going to press pause for a moment as an explanation is needed. To gain a full understanding of the two separate gospels, you must go to a book that provides a detailed explanation. I recommended three books in the Introduction which will assist your understanding. Israel's history is recorded in the Old Testament. It shows Israel having faith; then losing it. They follow God; then turn away from Him. <u>Under the Gospel of the Kingdom, they must have faith and maintain it. If they believe and continue in their faith, their sins will be forgiven by their Messiah at His return</u>. More evidence will be presented in the Gospel of Matthew that will support this. Some people may be upset that I do not take the time here to present the Gospel of Grace. I am maintaining my commitment to providing a commentary on the Gospel of Matthew. *The Hidden Gospel* is a short book dedicated to answering questions concerning the Gospel of Grace.

Christ continues teaching about believers who are fakes or insincere. What they do, they do for show. Yet, the Lord knows their hearts. Verses 16-18:

16 Moreover when ye fast, be not, as the hypocrites, of a sad countenance: for they disfigure their faces, that they may appear unto men to fast. Verily I say unto you, They have their reward.

17 But thou, when thou fastest, anoint thine head, and wash thy face; 18 That thou appear not unto men to fast, but unto thy Father which is in secret: and thy Father, which seeth in secret, shall reward thee openly.

There is a saying that where a man's heart is, there is his treasure also. The material things of earth are temporary, but the eternal things of God last forever. Verses 19-21:

19 Lay not up for yourselves treasures upon earth, where moth and rust doth corrupt, and where thieves break through and steal:

20 But lay up for yourselves treasures in heaven, where neither moth nor rust doth corrupt, and where thieves do not break through nor steal: 21 <u>For where your treasure is, there will your heart be also.</u>

48

It is said that the eyes are the mirror of the soul. What we see with our eyes reflects the desires of our heart. If we single-mindedly seek light, then our body is filled with light. Conversely, if we seek darkness, our body is filled with darkness. Verses 22-23:

> 22 **The light of the body is the eye: if therefore thine eye be single, thy whole body shall be full of light.**
>
> 23 **But if thine eye be evil, thy whole body shall be full of darkness. If therefore the light that is in thee be darkness, how great is that darkness!**

In the following, we can see the conflict between good and evil; between serving God and serving Satan. The word "mammon" is defined as "riches; wealth; or the god of riches." Verse 24:

> 24 **No man can serve two masters: for either he will hate the one, and love the other; or else he will hold to the one, and despise the other. Ye cannot serve God and mammon.**

God wants from the Jews today the same thing He wanted in the Old Testament. He wants them to believe; to have faith. Similarly, He wants them to depend upon Him. Think of how God preserved and protected Israel in the Wilderness. Yet, Israel rebelled and lost faith in God's Word. They failed to depend upon Him until they had no other choice. It is still the same message. He speaks to them lovingly as His children. Verses 25-30:

25 **Therefore I say unto you, Take no thought for your life, what ye shall eat, or what ye shall drink; nor yet for your body, what ye shall put on. Is not the life more than meat, and the body than raiment?**

26 **Behold the fowls of the air: for they sow not, neither do they reap, nor gather into barns; yet your heavenly Father feedeth them. Are ye not much better than they?** 27 **Which of you by taking thought can add one cubit unto his stature?**

28 **And why take ye thought for raiment? Consider the lilies of the field, how they grow; they toil not, neither do they spin:** 29 **And yet I say unto you, That even Solomon in all his glory was not arrayed like one of these.**

30 Wherefore, if God so clothe the grass of the field, which to day is, and tomorrow is cast into the oven, shall he not much more clothe you, O ye of little faith?

Israel needs to learn to trust and depend upon their heavenly Father. Verses 31-32:

31 Therefore take no thought, saying, What shall we eat? or, What shall we drink? or, Wherewithal shall we be clothed? 32 (For after all these things do the Gentiles seek:) for your heavenly Father knoweth that ye have need of all these things.

If Israel is to forget their cares and worries, what then should they do? Verses 33-34:

33 But <u>seek ye first the kingdom of God, and his righteousness; and all these things shall be added unto you</u>.

34 Take therefore no thought for the morrow: for the morrow shall take thought for the things of itself. Sufficient unto the day is the evil thereof.

8

Matthew 7

As we begin this chapter, consider the following. Jesus is not teaching the Gentiles. He is teaching the Jews, the children of Abraham, about the coming Kingdom. This is the eternal kingdom that was promised to King David. It is an earthly kingdom with Jesus, the Son of David, ruling from Jerusalem on David's throne. Their future King is preparing them for their future destiny. They will be part of the righteous monarchy ruled by the righteous Son of God in the flesh. We must see this as a process leading to that end.

In the opening verse, I want you to think about a court that oversees this kingdom. It is regulated by God's Law that is fulfilled by loving God and loving mankind. However, should a person not live up to these expectations and fail, they will be judged according to a precedent which they themselves have established. Wait a minute! What does this mean? If someone judges another for doing something and then does it themselves, they can be judged by the precedent which they themselves established. This is brilliant! There is no need for God to judge them because they have already judged themself. Consider this as we read Matthew 7:1-2:

> 1 **Judge not, that ye be not judged.** 2 **For with what judgment ye judge, ye shall be judged: and with what measure ye mete [measure out], it shall be measured to you again.**

This actually ties into the prayer which Jesus taught them to ask God to forgive their sins as they forgive others. This is completely different from the Gospel of Grace taught to the Gentiles by the Apostle Paul.

The future King continues to teach His subjects applying the above to the following. Verses 3-6:

> 3 **And why beholdest thou the mote [spot] that is in thy brother's eye, but considerest not the beam [plank] that is in thine own eye?**
>
> 4 **Or how wilt thou say to thy brother, Let me pull out the mote out of thine**

54

eye; and, behold, a beam is in thine own eye? 5 Thou hypocrite, first cast out the beam out of thine own eye; and then shalt thou see clearly to cast out the mote out of thy brother's eye.

6 Give not that which is holy unto the dogs, neither cast ye your pearls before swine, lest they trample them under their feet, and turn again and rend [tear] you.

Notice that Jesus used the words "dogs" and "swine." During Jesus's earthly ministry, there is a true dichotomy. At this time, the world was divided into two contrasting parts. There were the Jews or the circumcision. And, there were Gentiles or the uncircumcision. The Apostle Paul wrote, " . . . Christ was a minister of the circumcision for the truth of God, to confirm the promises made unto the fathers " (Rom. 15:8). Later, he made a comparison of Gentiles before they were saved by the Gospel of Grace. Ephesians 2:11-12:

11 Wherefore remember, that ye being in time past Gentiles in the flesh, who are called Uncircumcision by that which is [those who are] called the Circumcision in the flesh made by hands;

12 That at that time ye were without Christ, being <u>aliens from the commonwealth of Israel</u>, and <u>strangers from the covenants of promise</u>, having no hope, and <u>without God in the world</u>:

Gentiles were "without God." During this Age of Law, this was their state. From the perspective of Jesus and the children of Abraham, they were heathen, unclean, and had no part in the commonwealth of Israel. The Gospel of Matthew was written during the Age of Law to those subject to the Mosaic and Davidic Covenants. Therefore, the Gospel of Matthew must be interpreted based upon the Age of Law.

We continue with Matthew 7:7-11:

7 Ask, and it shall be given [to] you; seek, and ye shall find; knock, and it shall be opened unto you: **8** For every one that asketh receiveth; and he that seeketh findeth; and to him that knocketh it shall be opened.

9 Or what man is there of you, whom if his son ask [for] bread, will he give him a stone? **10** Or if he ask [for] a fish, will he give him a serpent?

11 If ye then, being evil, know how to give good gifts unto your children, how much more shall your Father which is in heaven give good things to them that ask him?

Here we see it again. They are told by the future King that they must treat others as they themselves wish to be treated. Verse 12:

12 Therefore all things whatsoever ye would [desire] that men should do to you, do ye even so to them: for this is the law and the prophets.

Their future King is teaching the children of Abraham. Think of it as an advanced training class for their future responsibility. Not only is this about the Jews interaction between themselves, but also their future role as a "nation of priests." Priests are called to intercede between God and someone else. These are the words that God told Moses to tell the people. This has to do with the Mosaic Covenant. Notice that it is conditional. Exodus 19:5-6:

5 Now therefore, <u>if</u> ye will obey my voice indeed, and keep my covenant, <u>then</u> ye shall be a peculiar treasure unto me above all people: for all the earth is mine:

> 6 <u>And ye shall be unto me a kingdom of priests, and an holy nation.</u> These are the words which thou shalt speak unto the children of Israel.

Many Bible teachers and preachers include the Gentiles with the Jews. However, God chose Israel for a specific purpose concerning the eternal Kingdom.

Jesus taught by creating images that were familiar to those listening. He created pictures for them that were worth a thousand words. They are told that few will find the path to life. Most will follow the easy route to destruction. Matthew 7:13-14:

> 13 Enter ye in at the strait gate: for wide is the gate, and broad is the way, that leadeth to destruction, and many there be which go in thereat: 14 Because strait is the gate, and narrow is the way, which leadeth unto life, and few there be that find it.

Those who teach false doctrine can be identified by their actions which He calls their fruit. Verses 15-20:

> 15 Beware of false prophets, which come

to you in sheep's clothing, but inwardly they are ravening wolves. 16 Ye shall know them by their fruits. Do men gather grapes of thorns, or figs of thistles? 17 Even so every good tree bringeth forth good fruit; but a corrupt tree bringeth forth evil fruit.

18 A good tree cannot bring forth evil fruit, neither can a corrupt tree bring forth good fruit. 19 Every tree that bringeth not forth good fruit is hewn down, and cast into the fire. 20 Wherefore by their fruits ye shall know them.

Many of them are too busy appearing to be religious or pious. However, they are self-serving and work for recognition. Verses 21-23:

21 Not every one that saith unto me, Lord, Lord, shall enter into the kingdom of heaven; but he that doeth the will of my Father which is in heaven.

22 Many will say to me in that day, Lord, Lord, have we not prophesied in thy name? and in thy name have cast out devils? and in thy name done many wonderful works? 23 And then will I

profess unto them, I never knew you: depart from me, ye that work iniquity.

As the masses listened to their future King, He brings all this to a conclusion. Verses 24-29:

24 **Therefore whosoever heareth these sayings of mine, and doeth them, I will liken him unto a wise man, which built his house upon a rock:** 25 **And the rain descended, and the floods came, and the winds blew, and beat upon that house; and it fell not: for it was founded upon a rock.**

26 **And every one that heareth these sayings of mine, and doeth them not, shall be likened unto a foolish man, which built his house upon the sand:** 27 **And the rain descended, and the floods came, and the winds blew, and beat upon that house; and it fell: and great was the fall of it.**

28 **And it came to pass, when Jesus had ended these sayings, the people were astonished at his doctrine:** 29 **For he taught them as one having authority, and not as the scribes.**

9

Matthew 8

The Gospel of Matthew was written in the narrative style making it easy to understand. In it, Matthew shares the facts and events that happened while the Son of God was with them. The disciples walked many miles together in order to share the good news — Gospel of the Kingdom — with the lost children of Israel. Matthew 8:1-4:

> 1 **When he was come down from the mountain, great multitudes followed him.**
>
> 2 **And, behold, there came a leper and worshipped him, saying, Lord, if thou wilt, thou canst make me clean.** 3 **And Jesus put forth his hand, and touched him, saying, I will; be thou clean. And immediately his leprosy was cleansed.**

4 And Jesus saith unto him, See thou tell no man; but go thy way, shew thyself to the priest, and offer the gift that Moses commanded, for a testimony unto them.

The priests were to be God's intermediaries under the Mosaic Law. In this healing, Jesus made sure the requirements of the Mosaic Law were followed. He directed the man who had been healed to priests.

Capernaum was a city located on the shore of the Sea of Galilee. Jesus' reputation continued to grow by word of mouth. Verses 5-9:

5 And when Jesus was entered into Capernaum, there came unto him a centurion, beseeching him, 6 And saying, Lord, my servant lieth at home sick of the palsy, grievously tormented.

7 And Jesus saith unto him, I will come and heal him. 8 The centurion answered and said, Lord, I am not worthy that thou shouldest come under my roof: but speak the word only, and my servant shall be healed.

9 For I am a man under authority, having soldiers under me: and I say to this man,

Go, and he goeth; and to another, Come,
and he cometh; and to my servant, Do
this, and he doeth it.

Look at Jesus' reaction to the faith of the centurion.
Verse 10:

10 When Jesus heard it, he marvelled,
and said to them that followed, Verily I
say unto you, I have not found so great
faith, no, not in Israel.

The future King was overwhelmed by his faith
of one who was surely a Gentile. None of the Jews
He had met so far had this level of faith. The centurion was confident that all Jesus has to do was speak
a command and his servant would be healed. There
is no need for Jesus, as One of authority, to come in
person. All He had to do was speak it. This centurion
may represent the Gentiles who would enter the future Kingdom. However, many of the children of
Abraham do not believe and will not enter the Kingdom. Verses 11-13:

11 And I say unto you, That many shall
come from the east and west, and shall
sit down with Abraham, and Isaac, and
Jacob, in the kingdom of heaven.

12 But the children of the kingdom shall be cast out into outer darkness: there shall be weeping and gnashing of teeth.

13 And Jesus said unto the centurion, Go thy way; and as thou hast believed, so be it done unto thee. And his servant was healed in the selfsame [same] hour.

While they traveled together, they visited Peter's home. Matthew recalled what happened. Verses 14-15:

14 And when Jesus was come into Peter's house, he saw his wife's mother laid, and sick of a fever. **15** And he touched her hand, and the fever left her: and she arose, and ministered unto them.

That evening, when His location was known, many came to Him for help and He cared for them. Verses 16-17:

16 When the even [evening] was come, they brought unto him many that were possessed with devils: and he cast out the spirits with his word, and healed all that were sick:

17 That it might be fulfilled which was spoken by Esaias the prophet, saying, Himself took our infirmities, and bare our sicknesses.

He is referring to Isaiah 53. When you have time, I recommend you read it in its entirety. Remember, Isaiah was a prophet sent by God to the Jews. God was speaking to the Jews about the coming Messiah. It laid out His life as a suffering servant and, ultimately, a sacrifice for His people.

The word "disciple" refers to those being taught by a teacher. They were students of the discipline or teaching. Verses 18-22:

18 Now when Jesus saw great multitudes about him, he gave commandment to depart unto the other side.

19 And a certain scribe came, and said unto him, Master, I will follow thee whithersoever thou goest. 20 And Jesus saith unto him, The foxes have holes, and the birds of the air have nests; but the Son of man hath not where to lay his head.

21 And another of his disciples said unto

**him, Lord, suffer [allow] me first to go
and bury my father. 22 But Jesus said
unto him, Follow me; and let the dead
bury their dead.**

His words may have sounded callous, but Jesus' time
on earth was limited. Those who wanted to learn
from Him must make this their priority.

While on the shore of the Sea of Galilee, they
had access to ships. In order to be removed from the
crowds, Jesus would escape to the Sea to be alone
with His disciples. This body of water was subject to
violent storms. Verses 23-27:

**23 And when he was entered into a ship,
his disciples followed him. 24 And, behold, there arose a great tempest in the
sea, insomuch that the ship was covered
with the waves: but he was asleep.**

**25 And his disciples came to him, and
awoke him, saying, Lord, save us: we
perish. 26 And he saith unto them, Why
are ye fearful, O ye of little faith? Then
he arose, and rebuked the winds and
the sea; and there was a great calm.**

27 But the men marvelled, saying, What

manner of man is this, that even the winds and the sea obey him!

His disciples learned much by listening to Jesus, but also from observing Him. Sometimes, it is what we see people doing that speaks louder than their words.

They traveled from the northwestern part of the sea to its eastern part. Arriving there, they have a confrontation with two demon-possessed men who are also called devils. The demons knew that Jesus is the Son of God. Verses 28-29:

> **28 And when he was come to the other side into the country of the Gergesenes, there met him two possessed with devils, coming out of the tombs, exceeding fierce, so that no man might pass by that way.**

> **29 And, behold, they cried out, saying, What have we to do with thee, Jesus, thou Son of God? art thou come hither to torment us before the time?**

Those who are in the spiritual realm of darkness are not ignorant. They know Jesus. They know the prophecies and they know about the coming judgment where they will be tormented.

At the scene of this bizarre event, there were men tending this herd of pigs who stood and watched. Verses 30-33:

> 30 **And there was a good way off from them an herd of many swine feeding.**

> 31 **So the devils besought him, saying, If thou cast us out, suffer [allow] us to go away into the herd of swine. 32 And he said unto them, Go. And when they were come out, they went into the herd of swine: and, behold, the whole herd of swine ran violently down a steep place into the sea, and perished in the waters.**

> 33 **And they that kept them fled, and went their ways into the city, and told every thing, and what was befallen to the possessed of the devils.**

News of this spread quickly. Soon everyone came to see for themselves. There were two men, formerly possessed, and in the sea floated the dead carcasses of the swine. They could see the proof of this supernatural event. Yet, notice their reaction. In many of the places that Jesus traveled, this spirit of unbelief persisted. Verse 34:

> 34 **And, behold, the whole city came out to meet Jesus: and when they saw him, they besought [begged] him that he would depart out of their coasts.**

10

Matthew 9

There has always been opposition to God. From the very beginning, Satan has been the antagonist who seeks to derail God's plan for the Restoration of Creation. Those who serve Satan, the prince of darkness, are the powers, principalities, and rulers of darkness. Matthew 9:1-2:

> 1 **And he entered into a ship, and passed over, and came into his own city.**
>
> 2 **And, behold, they brought to him a man sick of the palsy, lying on a bed: and Jesus seeing their faith said unto the sick of the palsy; Son, be of good cheer; thy sins be forgiven thee.**

Many of the religious leaders of Israel were part of this opposition. They held to the letter of the Law and not its spiritual intent. Verses 3-8:

> 3 And, behold, certain of the scribes said within themselves, This man blasphemeth. 4 And Jesus knowing their thoughts said, Wherefore [Why] think ye evil in your hearts? 5 For whether [it] is easier, to say, Thy sins be forgiven thee; or to say, Arise, and walk?

> 6 But that ye may know that the Son of man hath power on earth to forgive sins, (then saith he to the sick of the palsy,) Arise, take up thy bed, and go unto thine house. 7 And he arose, and departed to his house.

> 8 But when the multitudes saw it, they marvelled, and glorified God, which had given such power unto men.

Here, the writer of the Gospel of Matthew records his own recruitment. Verse 9:

> 9 And as Jesus passed forth from thence, he saw a man, named Matthew, sitting at the receipt of custom: and he saith unto him, Follow me. And he arose, and followed him.

72

Jesus was sitting and having a meal with those who the established religious leaders would consider to be unsavory characters. The word "publican" means "a collector of tolls or tributes." They may have been friends of Matthew who was himself a tax collector. Verses 10-12:

> 10 **And it came to pass, as Jesus sat at meat in the house, behold, many publicans and sinners came and sat down with him and his disciples.**
>
> 11 **And when the Pharisees saw it, they said unto his disciples, Why eateth your Master with publicans and sinners?**
>
> 12 **But when Jesus heard that, he said unto them, They that be whole need not a physician, but they that are sick.**

Jesus' remark go right to the point. The Pharisees had missed the intent of the Law. So, He directed them to go to the Scriptures to see that God desires "mercy, and not sacrifice." Verse 13:

> 13 **But go ye and learn what that meaneth, I will have mercy, and not sacrifice: for I am not come to call the righteous, but sinners to repentance.**

The Messiah did not come for those who are self-righteous and have no need for a Savior. He came for those who know that they are sinners and are in need of a Savior.

John the Baptist had his own students or disciples whom he taught. They compared what they were taught with what Jesus' disciples were doing. They wanted to know why there was a difference. Verse 14-15:

> 14 **Then came to him the disciples of John, saying, Why do we and the Pharisees fast oft, but thy disciples fast not?**

> 15 **And Jesus said unto them, Can the children of the bridechamber mourn, as long as the bridegroom is with them? but the days will come, when the bridegroom shall be taken from them, and then shall they fast.**

After answering their specific question, I believe that there was a larger group of people gathered. Jesus continued teaching in his usual style. Verses 16-17:

> 16 **No man putteth a piece of new cloth unto an old garment, for that which is**

put in to fill it up taketh from the garment, and the rent [tear] is made worse.

17 Neither do men put new wine into old bottles: else the bottles break, and the wine runneth out, and the bottles perish: but they put new wine into new bottles, and both are preserved.

While teaching, He was interrupted by two people in need of His help. Verses 18-26:

18 While he spake these things unto them, behold, there came a certain ruler, and worshipped him, saying, My daughter is even now dead: but come and lay thy hand upon her, and she shall live. 19 And Jesus arose, and followed him, and so did his disciples.

20 And, behold, a woman, which was diseased with an issue of blood twelve years, came behind him, and touched the hem of his garment: 21 For she said within herself, If I may but touch his garment, I shall be whole. 22 But Jesus turned him about, and when he saw her, he said, Daughter, be of good comfort; thy faith hath made thee whole. And

the woman was made whole from that hour.

23 And when Jesus came into the ruler's house, and saw the minstrels and the people making a noise, 24 He said unto them, Give place [Make room]: for the maid is not dead, but sleepeth. And they laughed him to scorn.

25 But when the people were put forth, [out] he went in, and took her by the hand, and the maid arose. 26 And the fame hereof went abroad into all that land.

In the 1980's, I commuted to work on Route 128 which encircles metropolitan Boston. During the rush hour commute, I would drive under a black iron railroad bridge. On it, there were in large letters spray-painted FAITH IS THE MIRACLE. That has always stuck in my mind. Faith is believing God.

Jesus moved on. Again, He was followed by those in need of His help. Verses 27-30:

27 And when Jesus departed thence, two blind men followed him, crying, and saying, <u>Thou Son of David</u>, have mercy

on us. 28 And when he was come into the house, the blind men came to him: and Jesus saith unto them, Believe ye that I am able to do this? They said unto him, Yea, Lord.

29 Then touched he their eyes, saying, According to your faith be it unto you. 30 And their eyes were opened; and Jesus straitly charged them, saying, See that no man know it.

After He healed them, He asked them to keep it to themselves. However, it may have been their joy, but they could not keep silent. Verse 31:

31 But they, when they were departed, spread abroad his fame in all that country.

Jesus must deal with another man possessed by an evil spirit. As the word "deaf" means "someone who cannot hear," the word "dumb" means "someone who is unable to speak." Verses 32-33:

32 As they went out, behold, they brought to him a dumb man possessed with a devil.

33 And when the devil was cast out, the dumb spake: and the multitudes marvelled, saying, It was never so seen in Israel.

The ever-present religious leaders stood and observed the miracle. Then, they accused Jesus of casting out the demon by the power of "the prince of the devils." They did not realize that they were judging the Son of God. They had accused Jesus of serving Satan, the prince of demons. Verse 34:

34 But the Pharisees said, He casteth out devils through the prince of the devils.

Matthew only records a few of many miracles performed by Jesus among His people. He tells us that the future King moved throughout the cities and towns. Wherever He went He preached and healed the sick. Verse 35:

35 And Jesus went about all the cities and villages, teaching in their synagogues, and preaching <u>the gospel of the kingdom</u>, and healing every sickness and every disease among the people.

At times, Jesus was concerned knowing how short His time would be with His people. His ministry would last only three years before He would be taken from them. Verses 36-38:

> 36 But when he saw the multitudes, he was moved with compassion on them, because they fainted, and were scattered abroad, as sheep having no shepherd.

> 37 Then saith he unto his disciples, The harvest truly is plenteous, but the labourers are few;

> 38 Pray ye therefore the Lord of the harvest, that he will send forth labourers into his harvest.

11

Matthew 10

Jesus saw the overwhelming need and knew the brevity of His time with His people. He empowered the Twelve to assist Him. Here, we see what they now could do. Matthew 10:1:

> 1 **And when he had called unto him his twelve disciples, he gave them power against unclean spirits, to cast them out, and to heal all manner of sickness and all manner of disease.**

Matthew provides a list of the Twelve. Verses 2-4:

> 2 **Now the names of the twelve apostles are these; The first, Simon, who is called Peter, and Andrew his brother; James the son of Zebedee, and John his brother;**

3 Philip, and Bartholomew; Thomas, and Matthew the publican; James the son of Alphaeus, and Lebbaeus, whose surname was Thaddaeus; 4 Simon the Canaanite, and Judas Iscariot, who also betrayed him.

The following verses are important as they prove the unique gospel message with which they were sent. Furthermore, it identifies the specific recipients to whom the Gospel of the Kingdom was to be delivered. Here are Christ's instructions to His Twelve. Verses 5-6:

5 These twelve Jesus sent forth, and commanded them, saying, <u>Go not into the way of the Gentiles</u>, and into any city of the Samaritans enter ye not: 6 <u>But go rather to the lost sheep of the house of Israel</u>.

They are to take <u>the Gospel of the Kingdom to the children of Abraham</u>. This is the good news of the imminent fulfillment of the kingdom promised to King David. Verse 7:

7 And as ye go, preach, saying, <u>The kingdom of heaven is at hand</u>.

As the disciples preach, they are now able to do miracles. These are their credentials and the Jews will know that these disciples represent the Messiah. He continues. Verses 8-15:

8 Heal the sick, cleanse the lepers, raise the dead, cast out devils: freely ye have received, freely give.

9 Provide neither gold, nor silver, nor brass in your purses, 10 Nor scrip for your journey, neither two coats, neither shoes, nor yet staves: for the workman is worthy of his meat.

11 And into whatsoever city or town ye shall enter, enquire who in it is worthy; and there abide till ye go thence. 12 And when ye come into an house, salute it. 13 And if the house be worthy, let your peace come upon it: but if it be not worthy, let your peace return to you.

14 And whosoever shall not receive you, nor hear your words, when ye depart out of that house or city, shake off the dust of your feet. 15 Verily I say unto you, It shall be more tolerable for the land of Sodom and Gomorrha in the

day of judgment, than for that city.

Their journey would not be without danger. The adversary and his dominion were watching. The Apostles' commission was not for the short term, but rather for the remainder of their life. Verse 16:

16 **Behold, I send you forth as sheep in the midst of wolves: be ye therefore wise as serpents, and harmless as doves.**

They will be mistreated — especially by the religious opposition. The word "scourge" means "to punish with a vindictive affliction." Verses 17-20:

17 **But beware of men: for they will deliver you up to the councils, and they will scourge you in their synagogues; 18 And ye shall be brought before governors and kings for my sake, for a testimony against them and the Gentiles.**

19 **But when they deliver you up, take no thought how or what ye shall speak: for it shall be given you in that same hour what ye shall speak. 20 For it is not ye that speak, but the Spirit of your Father which speaketh in you.**

These warnings apply to the Twelve, but will also apply to those who follow them. Reading this, it becomes clear that much of this will take place during the Tribulation. At this time, the Tribulation and Kingdom were both imminent. Verses 21-23:

> 21 And the brother shall deliver up the brother to death, and the father the child: and the children shall rise up against their parents, and cause them to be put to death.
>
> 22 And ye shall be hated of all men for my name's sake: but he that endureth to the end shall be saved. 23 But when they persecute you in this city, flee ye into another: for verily I say unto you, Ye shall not have gone over the cities of Israel, till the Son of man be come.

The above verse refers to the Second Coming at the end of the Tribulation when the Messiah returns to the faithful Jews as their King.

This future King continues teaching His disciples. Now, they are Apostles. He has given them a message, instructions for its delivery and its intended recipients — the lost sheep of the house of Israel. Verses 24-28:

85

24 The disciple is not above his master, nor the servant above his lord. 25 It is enough for the disciple that he be as his master, and the servant as his lord. If they have called the master of the house Beelzebub, how much more shall they call them of his household?

26 Fear them not therefore: for there is nothing covered, that shall not be revealed; and [nothing] hid, that shall not be known. 27 What I tell you in darkness, that speak ye in light: and what ye hear in the ear, that preach ye upon the housetops.

28 And fear not them which kill the body, but are not able to kill the soul: but rather fear him which is able to destroy both soul and body in hell.

These Twelve would expand the ministry. They learned from Jesus and would teach what He taught them. Verses 29-42:

29 Are not two sparrows sold for a farthing? and one of them shall not fall on the ground without your Father [knowing].

30 But the very hairs of your head are all numbered. 31 Fear ye not therefore, ye are of more value than many sparrows.

32 Whosoever therefore shall confess me before men, him will I confess also before my Father which is in heaven. 33 But whosoever shall deny me before men, him will I also deny before my Father which is in heaven.

34 Think not that I am come to send peace on earth: I came not to send peace, but a sword. 35 For I am come to set a man at variance against his father, and the daughter against her mother, and the daughter in law against her mother in law. 36 And a man's foes shall be they [those] of his own household.

37 He that loveth father or mother more than me is not worthy of me: and he that loveth son or daughter more than me is not worthy of me. 38 And he that taketh not his cross, and followeth after me, is not worthy of me. 39 He that findeth his life shall lose it: and he that loseth his life for my sake shall find it.

40 He that receiveth you receiveth me, and he that receiveth me receiveth him that sent me. 41 He that receiveth a prophet in the name of a prophet shall receive a prophet's reward; and he that receiveth a righteous man in the name of a righteous man shall receive a righteous man's reward.

42 And whosoever shall give to drink unto one of these little ones a cup of cold water only in the name of a disciple, verily I say unto you, he shall in no wise lose his reward.

These rewards will be distributed to those who deserve them when the Lord returns.

12

Matthew 11

Jesus continued teaching His Twelve, but now with their help, they could concentrate on reaching "the lost sheep of the house of Israel" (Matt. 10:6). Matthew 11:1:

1 **And it came to pass, when Jesus had made an end of commanding his twelve disciples, he departed thence to teach and to preach in their cities.**

John the Baptist sent two of his disciples to Jesus to ask Him if He was the Christ. Notice His response. Verses 2-6:

2 **Now when John had heard in the prison the works of Christ, he sent two of his disciples,** 3 **And said unto him, Art thou he that should come, or do we**

look for another?

4 Jesus answered and said unto them, Go and shew John again those things which ye do hear and see: 5 The blind receive their sight, and the lame walk, the lepers are cleansed, and the deaf hear, the dead are raised up, and the poor have the gospel preached to them.

6 And blessed is he, whosoever shall not be offended in [by] me.

Jesus continued to teach the multitudes who came to hear him. He began to speak about John the Baptist of whom Isaiah wrote, "The voice of him that crieth in the wilderness, Prepare ye the way of the LORD, make straight in the desert a highway for our God" (Isa. 40:3). The people had no doubt seen John's disciples who just left. Verses 7-15:

7 And as they departed, Jesus began to say unto the multitudes concerning John [the Baptist], What went ye out into the wilderness to see? A reed shaken with the wind?

8 But what went ye out for to see? A man clothed in soft raiment? behold, they

that wear soft clothing are in kings' houses.

9 But what went ye out for to see? A prophet? yea, I say unto you, and more than a prophet. 10 For this is he, of whom it is written, Behold, I send my messenger before thy face, which shall prepare thy way before thee.

11 Verily I say unto you, Among them that are born of women there hath not risen a greater than John the Baptist: notwithstanding he that is least in the kingdom of heaven is greater than he.

12 And from the days of John the Baptist until now the kingdom of heaven suffereth violence, and the violent take it by force. 13 For all the prophets and the law prophesied until John.

14 And if ye will receive it, this is Elias, which was for to come. 15 He that hath ears to hear, let him hear.

Jesus speaks about the current generation of Jews. This present generation was able to witness Emmanual, God with us, walking among them. In

Eden, Adam and Eve " . . . heard the voice of the LORD God walking in the garden in the cool of the day" (Gen. 3:8). God was now walking upon His Creation once again. What He found was far from what He wanted. Verses 16-18:

> 16 **But whereunto shall I liken this generation? It is like unto children sitting in the markets, and calling unto their fellows,** 17 **And saying, We have piped unto you, and ye have not danced; we have mourned unto you, and ye have not lamented.**

> 18 **For John came neither eating nor drinking, and they say, He hath a devil.**

The Messiah is called the Son of Man, because He was also the Son of Adam. They found fault with Him not knowing Who He was. The word "upbraid" means "to severely reproach" or "treat with contempt." Verses 19-20:

> 19 **The Son of man came eating and drinking, and they say, Behold a man gluttonous, and a winebibber [drunkard], a friend of publicans and sinners. But wisdom is justified of [by] her children.**

20 Then began he to upbraid the cities wherein most of his mighty works were done, because they repented not:

These are the cities where miracles were performed. In one city, instead of welcoming Him, they asked Him to leave.

Jesus tells of the judgment these faithless cities will suffer in the day of judgment. Verses 21-24:

21 Woe unto thee, Chorazin! woe unto thee, Bethsaida! for if the mighty works, which were done in you, had been done in Tyre and Sidon, they would have repented long ago in sackcloth and ashes. **22** But I say unto you, It shall be more tolerable for Tyre and Sidon at the day of judgment, than for you.

23 And thou, Capernaum, which art exalted unto heaven, shalt be brought down to hell: for if the mighty works, which have been done in thee, had been done in Sodom, it would have remained until this day. **24** But I say unto you, That it shall be more tolerable for the land of Sodom in the day of judgment, than for thee.

These are the children of Abraham who will soon kill the Son of God. Abraham was called a friend of God because he believed God and his faith was counted to him as righteousness. God would not forget Abraham's love or the promises that He made to him. Verses 25-27:

> 25 At that time Jesus answered and said, I thank thee, O Father, Lord of heaven and earth, because thou hast hid these things from the wise and prudent, and hast revealed them unto babes.
>
> 26 Even so, Father: for so it seemed good in thy sight. 27 All things are delivered unto me of [by] my Father: and no man knoweth the Son, but the Father; neither knoweth any man the Father, save the Son, and he to whomsoever the Son will reveal him.

Jesus knew that the majority of Israel would reject Him. Nevertheless, the Son of God did what God sent Him to do. He presented the offer. Verses 28-30:

> 28 Come unto me, all ye that labour and are heavy laden, and I will give you rest.
>
> 29 Take my yoke upon you, and learn of

[from] me; for I am meek and lowly in heart: and ye shall find rest unto your souls. 30 For my yoke is easy, and my burden is light.

The Gospel of the Kingdom is being proclaimed to the Jews. It is different from the Gospel of Grace which will later be proclaimed by the Apostle Paul. Presently, it is the Age of Law. To be saved, the faithful Jews must (1) acknowledge that Jesus is their Messiah and the Son of God. (2) They must turn their lives back to God by repenting. For them, water baptism is a public demonstration of this change. (3) The Mosaic Law which was given to their fathers must be rigidly followed. And, finally, (4) they must keep their faith in God's Word by providing evidence of that faith by their good works.

Salvation through the Gospel of the Kingdom has conditions that must be met for Jews in order to receive their salvation upon the Messiah's return. Later, in Matthew 24, we will see that salvation will only be awarded to those who "endure until the end." You might be skeptical, but hold onto this in your mind. As we continue, we will see this more clearly in the chapters ahead.

13

Matthew 12

As previously taught, there is a difference between following the letter of the Law and the intent of the Law. The religious leaders were pious and had added to God's Law far greater requirements than those prescribed by Moses. In the following, we can see this. Matthew 12:1-9:

> 1 **At that time Jesus went on the sabbath day through the corn; and his disciples were an hungred, and began to pluck the ears of corn, and to eat. 2 But when the Pharisees saw it, they said unto him, Behold, thy disciples do that which is not lawful to do upon the sabbath day.**
>
> 3 **But he said unto them, Have ye not read what David did, when he was an hungred, and they that were with him;**

4 How he entered into the house of God, and did eat the shewbread, which was not lawful for him to eat, neither for them which were with him, but only for the priests?

5 Or have ye not read in the law, how that on the sabbath days the priests in the temple profane the sabbath, and are blameless? 6 But I say unto you, That in this place is one greater than the temple.

7 But if ye had known what this meaneth, I will have [desire] mercy, and not sacrifice, ye would not have condemned the guiltless.

8 For the Son of man is Lord even of the sabbath day. 9 And when he was departed thence, he went into their synagogue:

Jesus' going into the synagogue was good for the people attending, but it was like stirring up a bees' nest. It was the sabbath and I am sure the synagogue was full since their attendance was required by the Mosaic Law. Verses 10-13:

10 And, behold, there was a man which

had his hand withered. And they asked him, saying, Is it lawful to heal on the sabbath days? that they might accuse him.

11 And he said unto them, What man shall there be among you, that shall have one sheep, and if it fall into a pit on the sabbath day, will he not lay hold on it, and lift it out? 12 How much then is a man better than a sheep? Wherefore it is lawful to do well on the sabbath days.

13 Then saith he to the man, Stretch forth thine hand. And he stretched it forth; and it was restored whole, like as the other.

Remember, God desires mercy and not sacrifice. Doing good to this man with the withered hand was Jesus showing mercy and was consistent with the intent of the Mosaic Law. However, notice the response of the religious leaders. Matthew 12:14:

14 Then the Pharisees went out, and held a council against him, how they might destroy him.

Jesus' popularity with the multitudes would temporarily shield Him from any attempts on His life. Verses 15-16:

15 But when Jesus knew it, he withdrew himself from thence: and great multitudes followed him, and he healed them all; 16 And charged them that they should not make him known:

Everything that Jesus did was done publicly and to fulfill the prophecies made by God through Israel's prophets. Verses 17-21:

17 That it might be fulfilled which was spoken by Esaias the prophet, saying,

18 Behold my servant, whom I have chosen; my beloved, in whom my soul is well pleased: I will put my spirit upon him, and he shall shew judgment to the Gentiles.

19 He shall not strive, nor cry; neither shall any man hear his voice in the streets.

20 A bruised reed shall he not break, and smoking flax shall he not quench, till he

**send forth judgment unto victory. 21
And in his name shall the Gentiles
trust.**

The other nations, non-Jews, also saw what was happening. Paul described the state of the Gentiles during the Age of Law. He said they were "aliens from the commonwealth of Israel, and strangers from the covenants of promise, having no hope, and without God in the world" (Eph. 2:12). This was true, but nevertheless, all the nations were watching.

The religious leaders actually accused the Messiah of operating under the powers of Satan. Consider the irony of this event. Verses 22-30:

22 Then was brought unto him one possessed with a devil, blind, and dumb: and he healed him, insomuch that the blind and dumb both spake and saw.

23 And all the people were amazed, and said, Is not this the son of David? 24 But when the Pharisees heard it, they said, This fellow doth not cast out devils, but by Beelzebub the prince of the devils.

25 And Jesus knew their thoughts, and said unto them, Every kingdom divided

against itself is brought to desolation; and every city or house divided against itself shall not stand: 26 And if Satan cast out Satan, he is divided against himself; how shall then his kingdom stand?

27 And if I by Beelzebub cast out devils, by whom do your children cast them out? therefore they shall be your judges.

28 But if I cast out devils by the Spirit of God, then the kingdom of God is come unto you. 29 Or else how can one enter into a strong man's house, and spoil his goods, except he first bind the strong man? and then he will spoil his house.

30 He that is not with me is against me; and he that gathereth not with me scattereth abroad.

This confrontation was between the religious leaders and the future King. Jesus, speaking as a prophet, makes an important proclamation that will soon affect Israel's immediate future. Verses 31-32:

31 Wherefore I say unto you, <u>All manner of sin and blasphemy shall be forgiven</u>

unto men: but the blasphemy against the Holy Ghost shall not be forgiven unto men.

32 **And whosoever speaketh a word against the Son of man, it shall be forgiven him: but whosoever speaketh against the Holy Ghost, it shall not be forgiven him, neither in this world, neither in the world to come.**

This was a powerful statement and worth remembering. It will play a critical part in the temporary suspension of the Age of Law described in the book of Acts.

Similar to parables as a teaching method, Jesus uses figurative language to make His point. He is speaking about Israel as a fruit tree. The quality of the fruit is determined by the quality of the tree. If the tree is bad, then the fruit it produces will also be bad. Verse 33:

33 **Either make the tree good, and his fruit good; or else make the tree corrupt, and his fruit corrupt: for the tree is known by his fruit.**

He continues by directing His comments to the religious leaders. Verses 34-37:

> 34 O generation of vipers, how can ye, being evil, speak good things? for out of the abundance of the heart the mouth speaketh.

> 35 A good man out of the good treasure of the heart bringeth forth good things: and an evil man out of the evil treasure bringeth forth evil things.

> 36 But I say unto you, That every idle word that men shall speak, they shall give account thereof in the day of judgment. 37 For by thy words thou shalt be justified, and by thy words thou shalt be condemned.

It is unlikely that the Pharisees are asking a sincere question. They were taunting Him to prove Himself. They had already seen Him performed miracles. However, without faith, they would not understand. Verse 38:

> 38 Then certain of the scribes and of the Pharisees answered, saying, Master, we would see a sign from thee.

Here is Jesus' response. Verses 39-42:

39 But he answered and said unto them, An evil and adulterous generation seeketh after a sign; and there shall no sign be given to it, but the sign of the prophet Jonas:

40 For as Jonas was three days and three nights in the whale's belly; so shall the Son of man be three days and three nights in the heart of the earth.

41 The men of Nineveh shall rise in judgment with [against] this generation, and shall condemn it: because they [the Ninevites] repented at the preaching of Jonas; and, behold, a greater [One] than Jonas is here.

42 The queen of the south shall rise up in the judgment with [against] this generation, and shall condemn it: for she came from the uttermost parts of the earth to hear the wisdom of Solomon; and, behold, a [Someone] greater than Solomon is here.

Many in Israel were possessed by unclean

spirits or demons. Jesus points out how a newly vacated home can be easily filled. Verses 43-45:

> 43 When the unclean spirit is gone out of a man, he [the demon] walketh through dry places, seeking rest, and findeth none.

> 44 Then he saith, I will return into my house from whence I came out; and when he is come, he findeth it empty, swept, and garnished [decorated}.

> 45 Then goeth he, and taketh with himself seven other spirits more wicked than himself, and they enter in and dwell there: and the last state of that man is worse than the first. Even so shall it be also unto this wicked generation.

While Jesus taught in the synagogue at length, His human family arrived outside. He was informed of their arrival. Verses 46-47:

> 46 While he yet talked to the people, behold, his mother and his brethren stood without, desiring to speak with him. 47 Then one said unto him, Behold, thy

mother and thy brethren stand without, desiring to speak with thee.

From Jesus' response, we find that believers had replaced His biological family. Verses 48-49

> 48 But he answered and said unto him that told him, Who is my mother? and who are my brethren?

> 49 And he stretched forth his hand toward his disciples, and said, Behold my mother and my brethren!

He goes on to say that anyone who does the will of His heavenly Father is His family. Verse 50:

> 50 For whosoever shall do the will of my Father which is in heaven, the same is my brother, and sister, and mother.

14

Matthew 13 (Part I)

News of Jesus' location spread far and wide. A large crowd gathered on the shore. Matthew 13:1-2:

> 1 **The same day went Jesus out of the house, and sat by the sea side.** 2 **And great multitudes were gathered together unto him, so that he went into a ship, and sat; and the whole multitude stood on the shore.**

Jesus adapted His teaching style to reach a broad spectrum of His listeners. As we read about them, there is one thing we must do. We must remember the context! Here we have the Jewish Messiah Who came to fulfill the promises made to the fathers. (See Rom. 15:8.) This Messiah brought them good news about the kingdom God promised to King David. The gospel message is this Kingdom is "at hand." Its arrival is imminent. Israel's future King is with them. This is truly good news! We will see this scenario play out.

The word "parable" comes from the Latin word which means "easily procured." It is a form of teaching that everyone can understand because it is a story. It is done by making a comparison to something familiar to the listeners. Some parables taught deep theological ideas so that even the disciples would later ask for an explanation. Before we move on, consider something previously mentioned in Matthew 9:37-38:

> 37 **Then saith he unto his disciples, <u>The harvest truly is plenteous</u>, but the labourers are few; 38 Pray ye therefore [to] <u>the Lord of the harvest</u>, that he will send forth labourers <u>into his harvest</u>.**

We can now continue. Matthew 13:3-9:

> 3 **And he spake many things unto them in parables, saying, Behold, a sower went forth to sow;**
>
> 4 **And when he sowed, some seeds fell by the way side, and the fowls came and**

devoured them up:

5 Some fell upon stony places, where they had not much earth: and forthwith they sprung up, because they had no deepness of earth: 6 And when the sun was up, they were scorched; and because they had no root, they withered away.

7 And some fell among thorns; and the thorns sprung up, and choked them:

8 But other fell into good ground, and brought forth fruit, some an hundredfold, some sixtyfold, some thirtyfold. 9 Who hath ears to hear, let him hear.

Jesus spoke to His disciples' privately and explained this teaching. We see the reason why Jesus chose to reveal its meaning to them alone. Verses 10-13:

10 And the disciples came, and said unto him, Why speakest thou unto them in parables?

11 He answered and said unto them, Because it is given unto you to know the

mysteries of the kingdom of heaven, but to them it is not given.

12 For whosoever hath, to him shall be given, and he shall have more abundance: but whosoever hath not, from him shall be taken away even that he hath.

13 Therefore [it is for that reason] speak I to them in parables: because they seeing see not; and hearing they hear not, neither do they understand.

Isaiah foretold the condition of Israel in a prophecy. Their lack of understanding was due to hearing and seeing but not understanding due to their lack of faith. Since this is important, let us look at Isaiah 6:9-10:

9 And he said, Go, and tell this people, Hear ye indeed, but understand not; and see ye indeed, but perceive not.

10 Make the heart of this people fat, and make their ears heavy, and shut their eyes; lest they see with their eyes, and hear with their ears, and understand

**with their heart, and convert, and be
healed.**

Isaiah tells Israel that the heart plays an important
role. They must be open and responsive to God's
voice which is His Spirit and His Word. Similarly, the
Apostle Paul would later face opposition and disbe-
lief with his gospel message. 2 Corinthians 4:3-4:

> 3 **But if our gospel be hid, it is hid to
> them that are lost: 4 In whom the god of
> this world hath blinded the minds of
> them which believe not, lest the light of
> the glorious gospel of Christ, who is the
> image of God, should shine unto them.**

Jesus continues with an explanation to the
Twelve. He wants them to understand that this is a
spiritual battle. Matthew 13:14-15:

> 14 **And in them is fulfilled the prophecy
> of Esaias, which saith, By hearing ye
> shall hear, and shall not understand;
> and seeing ye shall see, and shall not
> perceive:**
>
> 15 **For this people's heart is waxed gross,
> and their ears are dull of hearing, and
> their eyes they have closed; lest at any**

time they should see with their eyes, and hear with their ears, and should understand with their heart, and should be converted, and I should heal them.

The Twelve are difference. They have seen and heard the truth from the son of God! Verses 16-17:

16 **But blessed are your eyes, for they see: and your ears, for they hear.** 17 For verily I say unto you, That many prophets and righteous men have desired to see those things which ye see, and have not seen them; and to hear those things which ye hear, and have not heard them.

For their benefit, Jesus takes the parable of the Sower and breaks it down for them privately. Verses 18-23:

18 **Hear ye therefore the parable of the sower.** 19 **When any one heareth the word of the kingdom, and understandeth it not, then cometh the wicked one, and catcheth away that which was sown in his heart. This is he which received seed by the way side.**

20 But he that received the seed into stony places, the same is he that heareth the word, and anon [immediately] with joy receiveth it; **21** Yet hath he not root in himself, but dureth [lasts] for a while: for [but] when tribulation or persecution ariseth because of the word, by and by he is offended.

22 He also that received seed among the thorns is he that heareth the word; and the care of this world, and the deceitfulness of riches, choke the word, and he becometh unfruitful.

23 But he that received seed into the good ground is he that heareth the word, and understandeth it; which also beareth fruit, and bringeth forth, some an hundredfold, some sixty, some thirty.

Few of those who heard this parable understood its meaning. They were an agrarian society and understood planting seeds and working against all odds to bring forth a harvest. In the spiritual sense, Jesus and the Twelve were doing the same thing with the Gospel of the Kingdom. They were planting the seed and hoping that the gospel message would take hold and grow. It would, but only if they had faith.

The first half of Matthew 13 presented a lot of information. We must keep in mind two things. First, Jesus was teaching the children of Abraham. Second, it must be seen in light of the coming eternal Kingdom. The fields were ripe for harvest. There is a Jewish holiday which centers around the harvest. It is call Pentecost. It is also known by its Jewish name: "The Festival of Firstfruits." This celebrates the early harvest which precedes the general harvest. Those firstfruits are dedicated to God and belong to Him. Such are those who first believe — whose seed had taken root.

In the next chapter, we will continue with the rest of Matthew 13.

15

Matthew 13 (Part II)

Jesus teaches the Twelve more about the opposition. Matthew 13:24-30:

24 **Another parable put he forth unto them, saying, The kingdom of heaven is likened unto a man which sowed good seed in his field:** 25 **But while men slept, his enemy came and sowed tares [weeds] among the wheat, and went his way.** 26 **But when the blade was sprung up, and brought forth fruit, then appeared the tares also.**

27 **So the servants of the householder came and said unto him, Sir, didst not thou sow good seed in thy field? from whence [where] then hath it [came the] tares [weeds]?**

28 He said unto them, An enemy hath done this. The servants said unto him, Wilt [Desire] thou then that we go and gather them up?

29 But he said, Nay; lest while ye gather up the tares, ye root up also the wheat with them.

30 Let both grow together until the harvest: and in the time of harvest I will say to the reapers, Gather ye together first the tares, and bind them in bundles to burn them: but gather the wheat into my barn.

Jesus is speaking about the coming judgment. Those who are unworthy, called "tares" or "weeds," will be bound and cast into the fire.

These parables develop the disciples' understanding of the coming earthly Kingdom. Jesus will sit upon the throne of David and rule from Jerusalem. Again, the Kingdom is mentioned in the following. Verses 31-32:

31 Another parable put he forth unto them, saying, The kingdom of heaven is like to a grain of mustard seed, which a man took, and sowed in his field:

32 Which indeed is the least [smallest] of all seeds: but when it is grown, it is the greatest among herbs, and becometh a tree, so that the birds of the air come and lodge in the branches thereof.

Like the mustard seed, although small, it brings forth a tree of great stature.

Here is another parable concerning the kingdom which Jesus taught the people, but explained it to His Twelve privately. Verses 33-43:

33 Another parable spake he unto them; The kingdom of heaven is like unto leaven, which a woman took, and hid in three measures of meal, till the whole was leavened.

34 All these things spake Jesus unto the multitude in parables; and without a parable spake he not unto them: 35 That it might be fulfilled which was spoken by the prophet, saying, I will open my mouth in parables; I will utter things which have been kept secret from the foundation of the world.

36 Then Jesus sent the multitude away, and went into the house: and his disciples came unto him, saying, Declare unto us the parable of the tares of the field.

37 He answered and said unto them, He that soweth the good seed is the Son of man; 38 The field is the world; the good seed are the children of the kingdom; but the tares are the children of the wicked one;

39 The enemy that sowed them is the devil; the harvest is the end of the world; and the reapers are the angels.

40 As therefore the tares are gathered and burned in the fire; so shall it be in the end of this world. 41 The Son of man shall send forth his angels, and they shall gather out of his kingdom all things that offend, and them which do iniquity; 42 And shall cast them into a furnace of fire: there shall be wailing and gnashing of teeth.

43 Then shall the righteous shine forth as the sun in the kingdom of their

Father. Who hath ears to hear, let him hear.

Jesus, the coming King, continues to teach about His eternal Kingdom. To follow are several parables. Verses 44-50:

44 Again, the kingdom of heaven is like unto treasure hid in a field; the which when a man hath found, he hideth, and for joy thereof goeth and selleth all that he hath, and buyeth that field.

45 Again, the kingdom of heaven is like unto a merchant man, seeking goodly pearls: 46 Who, when he had found one pearl of great price, went and sold all that he had, and bought it.

47 Again, the kingdom of heaven is like unto a net, that was cast into the sea, and gathered of every kind: 48 Which, when it was full, they drew to shore, and sat down, and gathered the good into vessels, but cast the bad away.

49 So shall it be at the end of the world: the angels shall come forth, and sever [cut] the wicked [away] from among the

just, 50 And shall cast them into the furnace of fire: there shall be wailing and
gnashing of teeth.

Jesus confirmed that His disciples understood what
He was teaching them. Verse 51:

51 Jesus saith unto them, Have ye understood all these things? They say unto
him, Yea, Lord.

A scribe who understands the truths about the
kingdom would be able to teach the treasures from
the Law, the Prophets, and the Writings. But, he is
also able to teach the treasures from the Gospel of the
Kingdom. Verse 52:

52 Then said he unto them, Therefore
every scribe which is instructed unto
the kingdom of heaven is like unto a
man that is an householder, which
bringeth forth out of his treasure things
new and old.

Jesus would teach at one place for a while and
then move to the next. His ministry would be only
three short years and He must press on. Verse 53:

53 And it came to pass, that when Jesus

had finished these parables, he departed thence.

He returned to Nazareth, His childhood home, where many were familiar with Him and His family. There, He entered the synagogue and He taught them. Verses 54-56:

54 And when he was come into his own country, he taught them in their synagogue, insomuch that they were astonished, and said, Whence hath this man this wisdom, and these mighty works?

55 Is not this the carpenter's son? is not his mother called Mary? and his brethren, James, and Joses, and Simon, and Judas? 56 And his sisters, are they not all with us? Whence then hath this man all these things?

Like many of the others, their hearts were hardened. Although they saw Him and heard Him speak, they did not understand. In fact, they were offended. Verse 57:

57 And they were offended in him. But Jesus said unto them, A prophet is not without honour, save in his own coun-

try, and in his own house.

Because of their lack of faith, Jesus did few miracles in their presence. Verse 58:

> 58 **And he did not [do] many mighty works there because of their unbelief.**

16

Matthew 14

Jesus' fame was no longer regional, but had spread throughout Israel. Herod, the son of the king who murdered the Jewish children under two years of age, was now reigning as king. Recently, he had John the Baptist bound, imprisoned, and beheaded. The fame of Jesus had come to his attention. Matthew 14:1-5

> 1 **At that time Herod the tetrarch heard of the fame of Jesus, 2 And said unto his servants, This is John the Baptist; he is risen from the dead; and therefore mighty works do shew forth themselves in him.**
>
> 3 **For Herod had laid hold on John, and bound him, and put him in prison for Herodias' sake, his brother Philip's wife**

4 For John said unto him, It is not lawful for thee to have her. 5 And when he would have put him to death, he feared the multitude, because they counted him as a prophet.

Herod was a shrewd tyrant. His concern was not that John was a prophet speaking for God. He feared John's popularity with the people. To follow are the circumstances by which he had John the Baptist killed. This allowed the matter to appear to be out of his hands. Verses 6-12:

6 But when Herod's birthday was kept, the daughter of Herodias danced before them, and pleased Herod. 7 Whereupon he promised with an oath to give her whatsoever she would ask.

8 And she, being before instructed of [by] her mother, said, Give me here John Baptist's head in a charger.

9 And the king was sorry: nevertheless for the oath's sake, and them which sat with him at meat, he commanded it to be given her.

10 And he sent, and beheaded John in

the prison. 11 And his head was brought in a charger, and given to the damsel: and she brought it to her mother.

12 And his disciples came, and took up the body, and buried it, and went and told Jesus.

John's disciples came to Jesus to tell him. This news affected Him and He desired to be alone for John was His cousin. His solitude did not last long because the people found Him. Verses 13-14:

13 When Jesus heard of it, he departed thence by ship into a desert [deserted] place apart: and when the people had heard thereof, they followed him on foot out of the cities.

14 And Jesus went forth, and saw a great multitude, and was moved with compassion toward them, and he healed their sick.

The place where Jesus went to be alone was a deserted place far from the towns and cities. Yet, the people stayed with him in spite of lack of food and drink. Verses 15-21:

15 And when it was evening, his disciples came to him, saying, This is a desert place, and the time is now past; send the multitude away, that they may go into the villages, and buy themselves victuals [food].

16 But Jesus said unto them, They need not depart; give ye them [food] to eat. 17 And they say unto him, We have here but five loaves, and two fishes.

18 He said, Bring them hither to me. 19 And he commanded the multitude to sit down on the grass, and took the five loaves, and the two fishes, and looking up to heaven, he blessed, and brake [broke it], and gave the loaves to his disciples, and the disciples to the multitude.

20 And they did all eat, and were filled: and they took up of the fragments that remained twelve baskets full. 21 And they that had eaten were about five thousand men, beside women and children.

The day was drawing to a close and twilight

was approaching. He desired that His Twelve to leave Him and He would dismiss the multitude. Verse 22:

> 22 **And straightway Jesus constrained [convinced] his disciples to get into a ship, and to go before [ahead of] him unto the other side, while he sent the multitudes away.**

Jesus needed alone time and a chance to commune with His Father. He was now separated from the Twelve. This may have been an opportunity to have their faith tested. You decide. Verses 23-24:

> 23 **And when he had sent the multitudes away, he went up into a mountain apart [alone] to pray: and when the evening was come, he was there alone. 24 But the ship was now in the midst of the sea, tossed with waves: for the wind was contrary [against them].**

It was common for the night to be divided into four watches where someone was awake and watching. Each watch consisted of three hours so the person on duty would be fresh and alert. The first watch began at dusk. There were two three-hour watches until midnight and another two from midnight to dawn or six o'clock. The following occurred during "the fourth watch" which was between three o'clock and dawn. Verses 25-33:

25 And in the fourth watch of the night Jesus went unto them, walking on the sea. 26 And when the disciples saw him walking on the sea, they were troubled, saying, It is a spirit; and they cried out for fear.

27 But straightway Jesus spake unto them, saying, Be of good cheer; it is I; be not afraid. 28 And Peter answered him and said, Lord, if it be thou, bid me come unto thee on the water.

29 And he said, Come. And when Peter was come down out of the ship, he walked on the water, to go to Jesus. 30 But when he saw the wind boisterous, he was afraid; and beginning to sink, he cried, saying, Lord, save me.

31 And immediately Jesus stretched forth his hand, and caught him, and said unto him, O thou of little faith, wherefore [why] didst thou doubt?

32 And when they were come into the ship, the wind ceased. **33** Then they that were in the ship came and worshipped him, saying, Of a truth <u>thou art the Son of God.</u>

All of this happened in the region of the Sea of Galilee. Refreshed by His solitude and reunited with His friends, they sailed to the northwest shore to Gennesaret which is near Capernaum. Verses 34-36:

34 And when they were gone over, they came into the land of Gennesaret.

35 And when the men of that place had knowledge of him, they sent out into all that country round about, and brought unto him all that were diseased; **36** And besought him that they might only touch the hem of his garment: and as many as touched were made perfectly whole.

17

Matthew 15

The religious leaders came from Jerusalem to question Jesus about the practices of His disciples. Why did they not follow the traditions? Jesus responded and it all comes down to this. Religion which includes customs and traditions are the product of men who created their own rules. In their own wisdom, they added to what God has already said. Matthew 15:1-9:

> 1 Then came to Jesus scribes and Pharisees, which were of [from] Jerusalem, saying, 2 Why do thy disciples transgress the tradition of the elders? for they wash not their hands when they eat bread.
>
> 3 But he answered and said unto them, Why do ye also transgress the com-

mandment of God by your tradition?

4 For God commanded, saying, Honour thy father and mother: and, He that curseth father or mother, let him die the death.

5 But ye say, Whosoever shall say to his father or his mother, It is a gift, by whatsoever thou mightest be profited by me; 6 And honour not his father or his mother, he shall be free. Thus have ye made the commandment of God of none effect by your tradition.

7 Ye hypocrites, well did Esaias prophesy of you, saying, 8 <u>This people draweth nigh unto me with their mouth, and honoureth me with their lips; but their heart is far from me.</u> 9 But in vain they do worship me, <u>teaching for doctrines the commandments of men.</u>

Jesus quoted Isaiah 29:13. The prophet Isaiah wrote those words over six hundred years earlier!. Yet, for many Jews, nothing had changed. Their words were lip service. It was for this reason that God would test the Jews before His Son would return to Israel. The seven-year period of testing is called "the time of Jacob's trouble" (Jer. 30:7). This testing is like a refiner's fire. In Matthew 24, Jesus states, "But he that shall endure unto the end, the same shall be saved" (Matt. 24:13). Only true Israel, the remnant, will keep the faith and make it to the end.

Jesus taught the people and what He said offended these religious leaders. Verse 10-14:

> 10 And he called the multitude, and said unto them, Hear, and understand: 11 Not that which goeth into the mouth defileth a man; but that which cometh out of the mouth, this defileth a man.

> 12 Then came his disciples, and said unto him, Knowest thou that the Pharisees were offended, after they heard this saying? 13 But he answered and said, Every plant, which my heavenly Father hath not planted, shall be rooted up.

> 14 Let them alone: they be blind leaders of the blind. And if the blind lead the blind, both shall fall into the ditch.

Here the ditch means more than a trench. It has eternal implications.

Peter asks Jesus to explain His statement much to Jesus' disappointment. Verses 15-20:

> 15 **Then answered Peter and said unto him, Declare unto us this parable.** 16 **And Jesus said, Are ye also yet without understanding?**
>
> 17 **Do not ye yet understand, that whatsoever entereth in at the mouth goeth into the belly, and is cast out into the draught?**
>
> 18 **But those things which proceed out of the mouth come forth from the heart; and they defile the man.** 19 **For out of the heart proceed evil thoughts, murders, adulteries, fornications, thefts, false witness, blasphemies:**
>
> 20 **These are the things which defile a man: but to eat with unwashen hands defileth not a man.**

Moving onto the next city, He and the Twelve encounter a Canaanite woman who was a Gentile.

Jesus confirms the exclusivity of His mission to "the lost sheep of the house of Israel." However, because of her faith, He makes an exception. Verses 21-28:

> **21 Then Jesus went thence, and departed into the coasts of Tyre and Sidon.**
>
> **22 And, behold, a woman of Canaan came out of the same coasts, and cried unto him, saying, Have mercy on me, O Lord, thou Son of David; my daughter is grievously vexed with a devil.**
>
> **23 But he answered her not a word. And his disciples came and besought him, saying, Send her away; for she crieth after us. 24 But he answered and said, <u>I am not sent but [except] unto the lost sheep of the house of Israel.</u>**
>
> **25 Then came she and worshipped him, saying, Lord, help me. 26 But he answered and said, It is not meet [acceptable] to take the children's bread, and to cast it to dogs.**
>
> **27 And she said, Truth, Lord: yet the dogs eat of the crumbs which fall from their masters' table.**

28 Then Jesus answered and said unto her, O woman, <u>great is thy faith</u>: be it unto thee even as thou wilt. And her daughter was made whole from that very hour.

Jesus left and headed towards the Sea of Galilee where He would again be met by a multitude of people. Verses 29-31:

29 And Jesus departed from thence, and came nigh [near] unto the sea of Galilee; and went up into a mountain, and sat down there.

30 And great multitudes came unto him, having with them those that were lame, blind, dumb, maimed, and many others, and cast them down at Jesus' feet; and he healed them:

31 Insomuch that the multitude wondered, when they saw the dumb to speak, the maimed to be whole, the lame to walk, and the blind to see: and they glorified the God of Israel.

After three days, this large group of people had remained with Him without food. He had compassion on them and would not send them away faint from their lack of food. Verse 32-39:

32 Then Jesus called his disciples unto him, and said, I have compassion on the multitude, because they continue with me now three days, and have nothing to eat: and I will not send them away fasting, lest they faint in the way.

33 And his disciples say unto him, Whence should we have so much bread in the wilderness, as to fill so great a multitude?

34 And Jesus saith unto them, How many loaves have ye? And they said, Seven, and a few little fishes.

35 And he commanded the multitude to sit down on the ground. 36 And he took the seven loaves and the fishes, and gave thanks, and brake them, and gave to his disciples, and the disciples to the multitude.

37 And they did all eat, and were filled: and they took up of the broken meat that was left seven baskets full. 38 And

they that did eat were four thousand men, beside [not including] women and children.

39 And he sent away the multitude, and took [a] ship, and came into the coasts of Magdala.

18

Matthew 16

There are two religious sects within the Jewish religious leaders. They are the Pharisees and the Sadducees. Their difference is in their belief concerning the resurrection. The former believe and the latter does not. We could say that they shared two things in common. They did share a distain for each other and for anyone who threatened their established religion. Matthew 16:1-3:

> 1 The Pharisees also with the Sadducees came, and tempting [testing] desired him that he would shew them a sign from heaven.
>
> 2 He answered and said unto them, When it is evening, ye say, It will be fair weather: for the sky is red. 3 And in the morning, It will be foul weather to day:

for the sky is red and lowring. O ye hypocrites, ye can discern the face of the
sky; but can ye not discern the signs of
the times?

Jesus tells them of a sign that they will completely miss. The sign will be His death, burial, and
resurrection. Contrary to what many believe, the
story of Jonah and the great fish is not a fable or fairy
tale. If it were, then would Jesus have used it as a
comparison to what would befall Him? However,
His reference still eludes many. Verse 4:

4 A wicked and adulterous generation
seeketh after a sign; and there shall no
sign be given unto it, but the sign of the
prophet Jonas. And he left them, and
departed.

They were without a supply of food. So, Jesus
used this as an opportunity to teach them more about
faith. Verses 5-12:

5 And when his disciples were come to
the other side, they had forgotten to
take bread.

6 Then Jesus said unto them, Take heed
and beware of the leaven of the Phari-

sees and of the Sadducees. 7 And they reasoned among themselves, saying, It is because we have taken no bread.

8 Which when Jesus perceived, he said unto them, O ye of little faith, why reason ye among yourselves, because ye have brought no bread? 9 Do ye not yet understand, neither remember the five loaves of the five thousand, and how many baskets ye took up?

10 Neither [forget] the seven loaves of the four thousand, and how many baskets ye took up? 11 How is it that ye do not understand that I spake it not to you concerning bread, that ye should beware of the leaven of the Pharisees and of the Sadducees?

12 Then understood they how that he bade them not beware of the leaven of bread, but of the doctrine of the Pharisees and of the Sadducees.

Traveling by boat on the Sea of Galilee had its benefits. It provided them with the ability to travel without the throng of people following them. Each time they traveled, they would arrive at a new location and have time before they were discovered by the crowds. During one of these quiet times, Jesus asked them an important question. Verses 13-18:

13 **When Jesus came into the coasts of Caesarea Philippi, he asked his disciples, saying, Whom do men say that I the Son of man am?**

14 **And they said, Some say that thou art John the Baptist: some, Elias; and others, Jeremias, or one of the prophets. 15 He saith unto them, But whom say ye that I am?**

16 **And Simon Peter answered and said, <u>Thou art the Christ, the Son of the living God</u>.**

17 **And Jesus answered and said unto him, Blessed art thou, Simon Barjona: for flesh and blood hath not revealed it unto thee, but my Father which is in heaven. 18 And I say also unto thee, That thou art Peter, and upon <u>this rock</u> I will build my church; and the gates of hell shall not prevail against it.**

Here, we must pause for a moment. First of all,

contrary to popular interpretation, Peter is not the foundation upon which the Church is built. The Greek name for Peter is "petros" which means "rock or stone." In the Greek New Testament text, the feminine form for the noun, "petra," is used. This can be seen as a reference not to a physical "rock" but a conceptual "foundation" upon which the Church is built. That conceptual idea has to do with the statement from Peter which is underlined above. How do we know this? It is the statement of faith for all Jews to make when they accept the Gospel of the Kingdom. They must confess Who Jesus is! <u>He is their Messiah and the Son of God!</u> By believing in Who Jesus is and being baptized they will receive "remission of sins." This "remission" is a temporary putting away and not forgiveness which is eradication. Forgiveness of sins for the Jews comes when their Messiah returns. We will confirm this again shortly.

Jesus is revealing to His Twelve Who He is. Up until then, they may have thought He was a great prophet like Elijah. After He finishes speaking to Peter, He commits this to their confidence. Verse 19-20:

> **19 And I will give unto thee the keys of the kingdom of heaven: and whatsoever thou shalt bind on earth shall be bound in heaven: and whatsoever thou shalt loose on earth shall be loosed in heav-**

en.

20 Then charged he his disciples that they should tell no man that he was Jesus the Christ [Anointed One].

This was the turning point in Jesus' ministry. He would need to prepare the Twelve for what will happen in the future. The Messiah came to accomplish the will of the Father. He remained committed to faithfully completing His mission.

Matthew summarizes what no doubt took weeks of private discussions during which I am sure there were lots of questions. Verse 21:

21 From that time forth began Jesus to shew unto his disciples, how that he must go unto Jerusalem, and suffer many things of [by] the elders and chief priests and scribes, and be killed, and be raised again the third day.

From Peter's reaction, we have some insight into what the Twelve thought before His announcement. Many Jews believed, from prophecy, that Jesus would free Israel from Roman oppression. His current office of Prophet would lead Him to be the Passover Lamb Who would take away their sins. It would

146

be later when He returns as their mighty King. Then, He will destroy Israel's enemies. But, He must first complete His ministry on earth. Verses 22-23:

> 22 Then Peter took him, and began to rebuke him, saying, Be it far from thee, Lord: this shall not be unto thee.

> 23 But he [Jesus] turned, and said unto Peter, Get thee behind me, Satan: thou art an offence unto me: for thou savourest not the things that be of God, but those that be of men.

Speaking privately with the Twelve, He knew that this would not be easy for them. They would go against the powers, principalities, and rulers of darkness. This was a spiritual battle they were fighting. People need to choose sides and that choice will have eternal consequences. Verses 24-28:

> 24 Then said Jesus unto his disciples, If any man will come after me, let him deny himself, and take up his cross, and follow me. 25 For whosoever will save his life shall lose it: and whosoever will lose his life for my sake shall find it.

> 26 For what is a man profited, if he shall

gain the whole world, and lose his own soul? or what shall a man give in exchange for his soul?

27 For the Son of man shall come in the glory of his Father with his angels; and then he shall reward every man according to his works.

28 Verily I say unto you, There be some standing here, which shall not taste of death, till they see the Son of man coming in his kingdom.

At this point in time, the Tribulation is imminent. It has to do with the 490-year timeline given to the Prophet Daniel. At the 483-year mark, the Anointed One Who is Christ will be cut off. The remaining seven-year period is called "Jacob's time of trouble." This is studied and explained in great detail in three of my books: *Letters To Theophilus*, *The Glorious Destiny of Israel*, and *The Hidden Gospel*. Certainly, by now, this timeline has expired. That would be true if it were not for God's "temporary suspension" of the timeline. The reason of this interruption is important for any student of the Bible.

19

Matthew 17

In Matthew's narrative, he describes Jesus' consecration. This was preparation for the completion of His earthly ministry. This is known as the Transfiguration. I look at it as a spiritual ceremony in preparation for His death. Only three of the Twelve were included as witnesses. Matthew 17:1-5:

> 1 **And after six days Jesus taketh Peter, James, and John his brother, and bringeth them up into an high mountain apart [alone],**

> 2 **And was transfigured before them: and his face did shine as the sun, and his raiment was white as the light.** 3 **And, behold, there appeared unto them Moses and Elias talking with him.**

4 Then answered Peter, and said unto Jesus, Lord, it is good for us to be here: if thou wilt, let us make here three tabernacles; one for thee, and one for Moses, and one for Elias.

5 While he yet spake, behold, a bright cloud overshadowed them: and behold a voice out of the cloud, which said, <u>This is my beloved Son, in whom I am well pleased; hear ye him.</u>

These three were not used to the supernatural although they had seen Jesus performing miracles. This was divine proof that Jesus is the Son of the Living God. They were overwhelmed with fear. Verse 6:

6 And when the disciples heard it, they fell on their face, and were sore afraid.

Jesus understood His friends and showed compassion on them. Verses 7-8:

7 And Jesus came and touched them, and said, Arise, and be not afraid.

8 And when they had lifted up their eyes, they saw no man, save [except] Jesus only.

He instructed them to keep this matter private and not to share it with anyone until after His Resurrection. Verse 9:

> 9 **And as they came down from the mountain, Jesus charged them, saying, Tell the vision to no man, until the Son of man be risen again from the dead.**

During His time with His Twelve, Jesus had hinted or alluded to His being taken away from them. Many Jews held to the common belief that Elijah must come before the Messiah. Witnessing His Transfiguration, they asked questions. Verses 10-13:

> 10 **And his disciples asked him, saying, Why then say the scribes that Elias must first come?**

> 11 **And Jesus answered and said unto them, Elias truly shall first come, and restore all things. 12 But I say unto you, That Elias is come already, and they knew him not, but have done unto him whatsoever they listed. Likewise shall also the Son of man suffer of [by] them.**

> 13 **Then the disciples understood that he spake unto them of John the Baptist.**

They returned to the other disciples and the crowd of people. His ministry continued as normal. Verses 14-18:

14 And when they were come to the multitude, there came to him a certain man, kneeling down to him, and saying, 15 Lord, have mercy on my son: for he is lunatick, and sore vexed: for ofttimes he falleth into the fire, and oft into the water. 16 And I brought him to thy disciples, and they could not cure him.

17 Then Jesus answered and said, O faithless and perverse generation, how long shall I be with you? how long shall I suffer you? bring him hither to me.

18 And Jesus rebuked the devil; and he departed out of him: and the child was cured from that very hour.

His disciples had not yet grasped the source of these manifestations. This was spiritual warfare. It can only be combatted with faith in the One Who is actually doing the work. Verses 19-21:

19 Then came the disciples to Jesus apart, and said, Why could not we cast

him out?

20 And Jesus said unto them, <u>Because of your unbelief</u>: for verily I say unto you, If ye have faith as [the size of] a grain of mustard seed, ye shall say unto this mountain, Remove hence to yonder place; and it shall remove; and nothing shall be impossible unto you.

21 Howbeit this kind goeth not out but by prayer and fasting.

The prayer was a request to God. The fasting only provided clarity of mind. It did not earn or achieve the healing. No one can earn God's grace.

He begins to teach the Twelve privately what will happen to Him. Verses 22-23:

22 And while they abode in Galilee, Jesus said unto them, The Son of man shall be betrayed into the hands of men: 23 And they shall kill him, and the third day he shall be raised again. And they were exceeding sorry.

Representatives of Rome collect tribute which is a form of tax. Everyone was expected to pay.

These men came and questioned Peter as to why Jesus did not pay the required tax. Verses 24-27:

> 24 And when they were come to Capernaum, they that [who] received tribute money came to Peter, and said, Doth not your master pay tribute?
>
> 25 He saith, Yes. And when he was come into the house, Jesus prevented [stopped] him, saying, What thinkest thou, Simon? of whom do the kings of the earth take custom or tribute? of their own children, or of strangers? 26 Peter saith unto him, Of strangers. Jesus saith unto him, Then are the children free.
>
> 27 Notwithstanding, lest we should offend them, go thou to the sea, and cast an hook, and take up the fish that first cometh up; and when thou hast opened his mouth, thou shalt find a piece of money: that take, and give [it] unto them for me and thee.

20

Matthew 18

Jesus continues teaching His disciples and answering their questions. Matthew 18:1-6:

1 **At the same time came the disciples unto Jesus, saying, Who is the greatest in the kingdom of heaven?**

2 **And Jesus called a little child unto him, and set him in the midst of them,** 3 **And said, Verily I say unto you, Except ye be converted, and become as little children, ye shall not enter into the kingdom of heaven.**

4 **Whosoever therefore shall humble himself as this little child, the same is greatest in the kingdom of heaven.** 5 **And whoso shall receive one such little**

child in my name receiveth me.

6 But whoso shall offend one of these little ones which believe in me, it were better for him that a millstone were hanged about his neck, and that he were drowned in the depth of the sea.

Today, many people in the world are easily offended. Someone becomes offended when another transgresses against them. God is offended by those who sin against Him. Jesus discusses offences in verses 7-10

7 Woe unto the world because of offences! for it must needs be that offences come; but woe to that man by whom the offence cometh!

8 Wherefore if thy hand or thy foot offend thee, cut them off, and cast them from thee: it is better for thee to enter into life halt [lame] or maimed, rather than having two hands or two feet to be cast into everlasting fire.

9 And if thine eye offend thee, pluck it out, and cast it from thee: it is better for thee to enter into life with one eye, rath-

er than having two eyes to be cast into hell fire.

10 Take heed that ye despise not one of these little ones; for I say unto you, That in heaven their angels do always behold the face of my Father which is in heaven.

There is a dichotomy within the children of Abraham. Some sheep love God and follow Him. Other sheep turn away from God. They despise the ways of God and fight against Him. Jesus came to save the lost sheep of Israel. The Gospel of the Kingdom offers them an opportunity to repent — to turn back to God. The choice is theirs alone to make. Verses 11-14:

11 For the Son of man is come to save that which was lost.

12 How think ye? if a man have an hundred sheep, and one of them be gone astray, doth he not leave the ninety and nine, and goeth into the mountains, and seeketh that which is gone astray?

13 And if so be that he find it, verily I say unto you, <u>he rejoiceth more of that</u>

<u>sheep, than of the ninety and nine which went not astray.</u>

14 Even so it is not the will of your Father which is in heaven, that one of these little ones should perish.

A Jew's compliance with the Law is affected by their relationship with God and their relationship with others. Verses 15-20:

15 Moreover if thy brother shall trespass against thee, go and tell him his fault between thee and him alone: if he shall hear thee, thou hast gained thy brother.

16 But if he will not hear thee, then take with thee one or two more, that in the mouth of two or three witnesses every word may be established.

17 And if he shall neglect to hear them, tell it unto the church [assembly]: but if he neglect to hear the church [assembly], let him be unto thee as an heathen man [unsaved] and a publican.

18 Verily I say unto you, Whatsoever ye shall bind on earth shall be bound in

158

heaven: and whatsoever ye shall loose on earth shall be loosed in heaven.

19 Again I say unto you, That if two of you shall agree on earth as touching any thing that they shall ask, it shall be done for them of [by] my Father which is in heaven. 20 For where two or three are gathered together in my name, there am I in the midst of them.

Hearing this, Peter came to Jesus with a question. Verses 21-22:

21 Then came Peter to him, and said, Lord, how oft shall my brother sin against me, and I forgive him? till seven times? 22 Jesus saith unto him, I say not unto thee, Until seven times: but, Until seventy times seven.

Teaching the crowd, Jesus gave them a parable about a rich king and his debtor. The issue is how the forgiven debtor treats someone who is his debtor. Verses 23-35:

23 Therefore is the kingdom of heaven likened unto a certain king, which would take account of his servants.

24 And when he had begun to reckon [accounts], one was brought unto him, which owed him ten thousand talents. 25 But forasmuch as he had not to pay, his lord commanded him to be sold, and his wife, and children, and all that he had, and payment to be made.

26 The servant therefore fell down, and worshipped him, saying, Lord, have patience with me, and I will pay thee all.

27 Then the lord of that servant was moved with compassion, and loosed him, and forgave him the debt.

28 But the same servant went out, and found one of his fellowservants, which owed him an hundred pence: and he laid hands on him, and took him by the throat, saying, Pay me that [what] thou owest.

29 And his fellowservant fell down at his feet, and besought him, saying, Have patience with me, and I will pay thee all. 30 And he would not: but went and cast him into prison, till he should pay the debt.

31 So when his fellowservants saw what was done, they were very sorry, and came and told unto their lord all that was done.

32 Then his lord, after that he had called him, said unto him, O thou wicked servant, I forgave thee all that debt, because thou desiredst me: 33 Shouldest not thou also have had compassion on thy fellowservant, even as I had pity on thee?

34 And his lord was wroth [angry], and delivered him to the tormentors, till he should pay all that was due unto him.

35 So likewise shall my heavenly Father do also unto you, if ye from your hearts forgive not every one his brother their trespasses.

Jesus' message is the same. The moral of this parable was included in the Lord's model prayer. The petitioners are to ask God to forgive their trespasses or sins in the same manner in which they forgive the trespasses of others. This condition applies to all who are saved by the Gospel of the Kingdom.

21

Matthew 19

Jesus traveled to the coasts of Judaea. There, He was greeted by crowds seeking His healing. Matthew 19:1-2:

> 1 **And it came to pass, that when Jesus had finished these sayings, he departed from Galilee, and came into the coasts of Judaea beyond Jordan; 2 And great multitudes followed him; and he healed them there.**

The religious leaders, aware of His popularity, also came to see Him and hear what He was teaching the people. Verses 3-9:

> 3 **The Pharisees also came unto him, tempting [testing] him, and saying unto him, Is it lawful for a man to put away**

his wife for every [any] cause?

4 And he answered and said unto them, Have ye not read, that he which made them at the beginning made them male and female, 5 And said, For this cause shall a man leave father and mother, and shall cleave to his wife: and they twain shall be one flesh?

6 Wherefore they are no more twain [two], but one flesh. What therefore God hath joined together, let not man put asunder.

7 They say unto him, Why did Moses then command to give a writing of divorcement, and to put her away?

8 He saith unto them, Moses because of the hardness of your hearts suffered [allowed] you to put away your wives: but from the beginning it was not so.

9 And I say unto you, Whosoever shall put away his wife, except it be for fornication, and shall marry another, committeth adultery: and whoso marrieth her which is put away doth commit a-

dultery.

His disciples would often ask Him questions privately for clarification. His response has to do with eunuchs who are males who were emasculated. Verses 10-12:

10 **His disciples say unto him, If the case of the man be so with his wife, it is not good to marry.**

11 **But he said unto them, All men cannot receive this saying, save [except] they to whom it is given. 12 For there are some eunuchs, which were so born from their mother's womb: and there are some eunuchs, which were made eunuchs of [by] men: and there be eunuchs, which have made themselves eunuchs for the kingdom of heaven's sake. He that is able to receive it, let him receive it.**

Jesus loves children because of their simplicity of mind and sincerity of heart. People brought their children to Him for His blessing. Since they were not sick or in need of healing like the others, the disciples reprimanded them. Verses 13-15:

13 Then were there brought unto him little children, that he should put his hands on them, and pray: and the disciples rebuked them.

14 But Jesus said, Suffer [Allow] little children, and forbid them not, to come unto me: for of such is the kingdom of heaven. 15 And he laid his hands on them, and departed thence.

Matthew records the interaction between Jesus and a young man asking, "What good thing shall I do?" Jesus responds, but in the end what He asked of him was too much because his riches on earth were great. Verses 16-22:

16 And, behold, one came and said unto him, Good Master, what good thing shall I do, that I may have eternal life? 17 And he said unto him, Why callest thou me good? there is none good but one, that is, God: but if thou wilt enter into life, keep the commandments.

18 He saith unto him, Which? Jesus said, Thou shalt do no murder, Thou shalt not commit adultery, Thou shalt not steal, Thou shalt not bear false witness,

19 Honour thy father and thy mother: and, Thou shalt love thy neighbour as thyself.

20 The young man saith unto him, All these things have I kept from my youth up: what lack I yet? 21 Jesus said unto him, If thou wilt be perfect, go and sell that [what] thou hast, and give to the poor, and thou shalt have treasure in heaven: and come and follow me.

22 But when the young man heard that saying, he went away sorrowful: for he had great possessions.

Jesus shared His thoughts with His disciples concerning this young man. Verses 23-26:

23 Then said Jesus unto his disciples, Verily I say unto you, That a rich man shall hardly enter into the kingdom of heaven. 24 And again I say unto you, It is easier for a camel to go through the eye of a needle, than for a rich man to enter into the kingdom of God.

25 When his disciples heard it, they were exceedingly amazed, saying, Who then

can be saved? 26 But Jesus beheld them, and said unto them, With men this is impossible; but with God all things are possible.

Peter speaks up and asks Jesus a question concerning all that they have given up to become His disciples. What shall they receive? Verses 27-30:

27 Then answered Peter and said unto him, Behold, we have forsaken all, and followed thee; what shall we have therefore?

28 And Jesus said unto them, Verily I say unto you, That ye which have followed me, in the regeneration when the Son of man shall sit in the throne of his glory, ye also shall sit upon twelve thrones, judging the twelve tribes of Israel.

29 And every one that hath forsaken houses, or brethren, or sisters, or father, or mother, or wife, or children, or lands, for my name's sake, shall receive an hundredfold, and shall inherit everlasting life.

30 But many that are first shall be last;

and the last shall be first.

Let us consider this last verse. It has to do with those who are alive at the time of His Coming. They were not the first to believe, but are alive when He returns. Therefore, they are the first. Those who first believed have died and are asleep at His Coming. They will be resurrected and will join the others last.

22

Matthew 20

Jesus speaks about those who are saved first and those who are saved last. Matthew 20:1-16:

1 **For the kingdom of heaven is like unto a man that is an householder, which went out early in the morning to hire labourers into his vineyard.**

2 **And when he had agreed with the labourers for a penny a day, he sent them into his vineyard.** 3 **And he went out about the third hour, and saw others standing idle in the marketplace,** 4 **And said unto them; Go ye also into the vineyard, and whatsoever is right I will give you. And they went their way.**

5 **Again he went out about the sixth and ninth hour, and did likewise.** 6 **And**

about the eleventh hour he went out, and found others standing idle, and saith unto them, Why stand ye here all the day idle? 7 They say unto him, Because no man hath hired us. He saith unto them, Go ye also into the vineyard; and whatsoever is right, that shall ye receive.

8 So when even [evening] was come, the lord of the vineyard saith unto his steward, Call the labourers, and give them their hire, beginning from the last unto the first. 9 And when they came that were hired about the eleventh hour, they received every man a penny. 10 But when the first came, they supposed that they should have received more; and they likewise received every man a penny.

11 And when they had received it, they murmured against the goodman of the house, 12 Saying, These last have wrought but one hour, and thou hast made them equal unto us, which have borne the burden and heat of the day.

13 But he answered one of them, and

said, Friend, I do thee no wrong: didst not thou agree with me for a penny? 14 Take that [which] thine is, and go thy way: I will give unto this last, even as unto thee. 15 Is it not lawful for me to do what I will with mine own? Is thine eye evil, because I am good?

16 **So the last shall be first, and the first last: for many be called, but few chosen.**

Many times we find references in the Bible to "going up" to Jerusalem because it is on a higher elevation than most of Israel. Planning His trip to Jerusalem, He takes His disciples aside. He desires for them to know what will befall Him and assures them it is according to God's will. Verses 17-19:

17 And Jesus going up to Jerusalem took the twelve disciples apart in [along] the way, and said unto them,

18 Behold, we go up to Jerusalem; and the Son of man shall be betrayed unto the chief priests and unto the scribes, and they shall condemn him to death,

19 And shall deliver him to the Gentiles to mock, and to scourge, and to crucify

him: and the third day he shall rise again.

Before they leave, the mother of James and John, sons of Zebedee, came to Jesus to make a request. Verses 20-28:

20 Then came to him the mother of Zebedee's children with her sons, worshipping him, and desiring a certain thing of him.

21 And he said unto her, What wilt thou? She saith unto him, Grant that these my two sons may sit, the one on thy right hand, and the other on the left, in thy kingdom.

22 But Jesus answered and said, Ye know not what ye ask. Are ye able to drink of the cup that I shall drink of, and to be baptized with the baptism that I am baptized with? They say unto him, We are able.

23 And he saith unto them, Ye shall drink indeed of my cup, and be baptized with the baptism that I am baptized with: but to sit on my right hand,

and on my left, is not mine to give, but it shall be given to them for whom it is prepared of [by] my Father.

24 And when the ten heard it, they were moved with indignation against the two brethren. 25 But Jesus called them unto him, and said, Ye know that the princes of the Gentiles exercise dominion over them, and they that are great exercise authority upon them.

26 But it shall not be so among you: but whosoever will be great among you, let him be your minister; 27 And whosoever will be chief among you, let him be your servant:

28 Even [That is to say] as the Son of man came not to be ministered unto, but to minister, and to give his life [as] a ransom for many.

Shortly after this, they begin their journey to Jerusalem by way of Jericho. Verse 29:

29 And as they departed from Jericho, a great multitude followed him.

As Jesus continued along the way, there were people traveling with Him. Two blind men called out to Him by His name "Son of David." Matthew began his gospel by establishing Jesus' geneaology to prove He was David's Son and the promised Messiah. Verses 30-34:

> 30 **And, behold, two blind men sitting by the way side, when they heard that Jesus passed by, cried out, saying, <u>Have mercy on us, O Lord, thou Son of David.</u>**
>
> 31 **And the multitude rebuked them, because they should hold their peace: but they cried the more, saying, <u>Have mercy on us, O Lord, thou Son of David.</u>**
>
> 32 **And Jesus stood still, and called them, and said, What will ye that I shall do unto you?** 33 **They say unto him, Lord, that our eyes may be opened.**
>
> 34 **So Jesus had compassion on them, and touched their eyes: and immediately their eyes received sight, and they followed him.**

23

Matthew 21

The Mount of Olives is located about two miles east of Jerusalem. It is a mountain ridge which is covered with olive trees. Here, Jesus stopped on His way. Certain things must be done in preparation for the Passover and Jesus began to make arrangements. Matthew 21:1-3:

1 And when they drew nigh unto Jerusalem, and were come to Bethphage, unto the mount of Olives, then sent Jesus two disciples,

2 Saying unto them, Go into the village over against you, and straightway ye shall find an ass tied, and a colt with her: loose them, and bring them unto me.

3 And if any man say ought unto you, ye shall say, The Lord hath need of them; and straightway he will send them.

There is a two-fold purpose for prophecy. First, it foretells of future events to either encourage or warn those who receive the prophecy. Second, in the future it confirms that what God said He will do, He is now doing. We see the providential nature of the actions surrounding the Messiah were foreordained. Verses 4-7:

4 All this was done, that it might be fulfilled which was spoken by the prophet, saying, **5** Tell ye the daughter of Sion, Behold, thy King cometh unto thee, meek, and sitting upon an ass, and a colt the foal of an ass.

6 And the disciples went, and did as Jesus commanded them, **7** And brought the ass, and the colt, and put on them their clothes, and they set him thereon.

Zechariah had written this prophecy some five hundred years earlier. Zechariah 9:9:

9 Rejoice greatly, O daughter of Zion; shout, O daughter of Jerusalem:

behold, thy King cometh unto thee:
he is just, and having salvation;
lowly, and riding upon an ass,
and upon a colt the foal of an ass.

News spread throughout the region and the streets of Jerusalem were jammed in anticipation. Matthew 21:8-11:

8 And a very great multitude spread their garments in the way; others cut down branches from the trees, and strawed them in the way.

9 And the multitudes that went before, and that followed, cried, saying, <u>Hosanna to the Son of David: Blessed is he that cometh in the name of the Lord; Hosanna in the highest.</u>

10 And when he was come into Jerusalem, all the city was moved, saying, Who is this? 11 And the multitude said, This is Jesus the prophet of Nazareth of Galilee.

In all the excitement, many did not know Him. Jesus had maintained a distance from Jerusalem. He knew He would not be welcomed by the religious leaders who claim to represent God. Verses 12-14:

> 12 And Jesus went into the temple of God, and cast out all them that sold and bought in the temple, and overthrew the tables of the moneychangers, and the seats of them that sold doves,

> 13 And said unto them, It is written, My house shall be called the house of prayer; but ye have made it a den of thieves.

> 14 And the blind and the lame came to him in the temple; and he healed them.

Here, we see the jealousy and indignation of the priests and scribes. Verses 15-16:

> 15 And when the chief priests and scribes saw the wonderful things that he did, and the children crying [aloud] in the temple, and saying, Hosanna to the Son of David; they were sore [very] displeased,

> 16 And said unto him, Hearest thou what these say? And Jesus saith unto them, Yea; have ye never read, Out of the

mouth of babes and sucklings thou hast perfected praise?

Here, Jesus departs from Jerusalem. He had accomplished what He wanted by figuratively knocking down the hornets' nest. Verse 17:

> 17 **And he left them, and went out of the city into Bethany; and he lodged there.**

In the gospels, Israel is often figuratively referred to as sheep, a vine, or a tree. This is because they are earthly-bound and needed nurturing by a shepherd or caretaker. The following is an analogy of Israel. It is about a fig tree which was not bearing the fruit that the Landowner expected. Verses 18-19:

> 18 **Now in the morning as he returned into the city, he hungered. 19 And when he saw a fig tree in the way, he came to it, and found nothing thereon, but leaves only, and said unto it, Let no fruit grow on thee henceforward for ever. And presently the fig tree withered away.**

His judgment was almost instant and it caused the disciples to wonder. Verses 20-22:

20 And when the disciples saw it, they marvelled, saying, How soon is the fig tree withered away!

21 Jesus answered and said unto them, Verily I say unto you, If ye have faith, and doubt not, ye shall not only do this which is done to the fig tree, but also if ye shall say unto this mountain, Be thou removed, and be thou cast into the sea; it shall be done.

22 And all things, whatsoever ye shall ask in prayer, believing, ye shall receive.

Since Jesus' time at the Temple the day before, the religious priests and elders debated the present situation. They came to see Jesus as He taught in the Temple. Verses 23-27:

23 And when he was come into the temple, the chief priests and the elders of the people came unto him as he was teaching, and said, By what authority doest thou these things? and who gave thee this authority?

24 And Jesus answered and said unto

them, I also will ask you one thing, which if ye tell me, I in like wise will tell you by what authority I do these things.

25 The baptism of John, whence was it? from heaven, or of men? And they reasoned with themselves, saying, If we shall say, From heaven; he will say unto us, Why did ye not then believe him? 26 But if we shall say, Of men; we fear the people; for all hold John as a prophet.

27 And they answered Jesus, and said, We cannot tell. And he said unto them, Neither tell I you by what authority I do these things.

Jesus presents a hypothetical situation to the priests. Then, He asks them for their opinion. Verses 28-32:

28 But what think ye? A certain man had two sons; and he came to the first, and said, Son, go work to day in my vineyard. 29 He answered and said, I will not: but afterward he repented, and went. 30 And he came to the second, and said likewise. And he answered and

said, I go, sir: and went not.

31 Whether of them twain [the two] did the will of his father? They say unto him, The first. Jesus saith unto them, Verily I say unto you, That the publicans and the harlots go into the kingdom of God before you.

32 For John came unto you in the way of righteousness, and ye believed him not: but the publicans and the harlots believed him: and ye, when ye had seen it, repented not afterward, that ye might believe him.

No one knows the Law better than the One Who created it. They were speechless, but Jesus continues. Verses 33-40:

33 Hear another parable: There was a certain householder, which planted a vineyard, and hedged it round about, and digged a winepress in it, and built a tower, and let it out to husbandmen, and went into a far country:

34 And when the time of the fruit [harvest] drew near, he sent his servants to

the husbandmen, that they might receive the fruits of it.

35 And the husbandmen took his servants, and beat one, and killed another, and stoned another. 36 Again, he sent other servants more than the first: and they did unto them likewise.

37 But last of all he sent unto them his son, saying, They will reverence my son. 38 But when the husbandmen saw the son, they said among themselves, This is the heir; come, let us kill him, and let us seize on his inheritance. 39 And they caught him, and cast him out of the vineyard, and slew him.

40 When the lord therefore of the vineyard cometh, what will he do unto those husbandmen?

In their answer, they would unknowingly be judging themselves. Verses 41-46:

41 They say unto him, He will miserably destroy those wicked men, and will let out his vineyard unto other husbandmen, which shall render him the fruits

in their seasons.

42 Jesus saith unto them, Did ye never read in the scriptures, The stone which the builders rejected, the same is become the head of the corner: this is the Lord's doing, and it is marvellous in our eyes?

43 Therefore say I unto you, The kingdom of God shall be taken from you, and given to a nation bringing forth the fruits thereof. 44 And whosoever shall fall on this stone shall be broken: but on whomsoever it shall fall, it will grind him to powder.

45 And when the chief priests and Pharisees had heard his parables, they perceived that he spake of [about] them. 46 But when they sought to lay hands on him, they feared the multitude, because they took him for a prophet.

24

Matthew 22

I would like to point out that, in the Gospel of Matthew, the word "kingdom" is used fifty-five times. Furthermore, the Jews are saved by the Gospel of the Kingdom. They will live on earth in the eternal Kingdom and serve under their eternal King Whose throne will be located in Jerusalem. They will have the Law written on their hearts and they will serve their King as a royal priesthood. This should be very exciting for the Jews! Jesus teaches them the nature of this Kingdom. Matthew 22:1-14:

1 **And Jesus answered and spake unto them again by parables, and said,**

2 **The kingdom of heaven is like unto a certain king, which made a marriage for his son,** 3 **And sent forth his servants to call them that were bidden to the wed-**

ding: and they would not come.

4 Again, he sent forth other servants, saying, Tell them which are bidden [invited], Behold, I have prepared my dinner: my oxen and my fatlings are killed, and all things are ready: come unto the marriage.

5 But they made light of it, and went their ways, one to his farm, another to his merchandise: 6 And the remnant took his [the king's] servants, and entreated them spitefully, and slew them.

7 But when the king heard thereof, he was wroth [angry]: and he sent forth his armies, and destroyed those murderers, and burned up their city.

8 Then saith he to his servants, The wedding is ready, but they which were bidden were not worthy.

9 Go ye therefore into the highways, and as many as ye shall find, bid [invite] to the marriage. 10 So those servants went out into the highways, and gathered together all as many as they found, both

bad and good: and the wedding was furnished with guests.

11 And when the king came in to see the guests, he saw there a man which had not on a wedding garment: 12 And he saith unto him, Friend, how camest thou in hither not having a wedding garment? And he was speechless.

13 Then said the king to the servants, Bind him hand and foot, and take him away, and cast him into outer darkness; there shall be weeping and gnashing of teeth. 14 For many are called, but few are chosen.

The Pharisees debated among themselves how they might trap Him in His words. They sent representatives out to question Him. Verses 15-22:

15 Then went the Pharisees, and took counsel how they might entangle him in his talk.

16 And they sent out unto him their disciples with the Herodians, saying, Master, we know that thou art true, and teachest the way of God in truth, neither

carest thou for any man: for thou regardest not the person of men.

17 Tell us therefore, What thinkest thou? Is it lawful to give tribute unto Caesar, or not?

18 But Jesus perceived their wickedness, and said, Why tempt [test] ye me, ye hypocrites? 19 Shew me the tribute money. And they brought unto him a penny. 20 And he saith unto them, Whose is this image and superscription? 21 They say unto him, Caesar's. Then saith he unto them, Render therefore unto Caesar the things which are Caesar's; and unto God the things that are God's.

22 When they had heard these words, they marvelled, and left him, and went their way.

Since their first attempt failed, others were sent to ensnare Him. Verses 23-33:

23 The same day came to him the Sadducees, which say that there is no resurrection, and asked him, 24 Saying, Master,

Moses said, If a man die, having no children, his brother shall marry his wife, and raise up seed unto his brother.

25 Now there were with us seven brethren: and the first, when he had married a wife, deceased, and, having no issue, left his wife unto his brother:

26 Likewise the second also, and the third, unto the seventh. 27 And last of all the woman died also. 28 Therefore in the resurrection whose wife shall she be of the seven? for they all had her.

29 Jesus answered and said unto them, Ye do err, not knowing the scriptures, nor the power of God.

30 For in the resurrection they neither marry, nor are given in marriage, but are as the angels of God in heaven. 31 But as touching the resurrection of the dead, have ye not read that which was spoken unto you by God, saying, 32 I am the God of Abraham, and the God of Isaac, and the God of Jacob? God is not the God of the dead, but of the living.

33 And when the multitude heard this, they were astonished at his doctrine.

The Sadducees had failed. Like a clique or a cabal, the Pharisees huddled together to assail Him with another question. How futile this was as they debated the future King. Verse 34-40:

34 But when the Pharisees had heard that he had put the Sadducees to silence, they were gathered together.

35 Then one of them, which was a lawyer, asked him a question, tempting [testing] him, and saying, **36** Master, which is the great commandment in the law?

37 Jesus said unto him, Thou shalt love the Lord thy God with all thy heart, and with all thy soul, and with all thy mind. **38** This is the first and great commandment. **39** And the second is like unto it, Thou shalt love thy neighbour as thyself.

40 On these two commandments hang all the law and the prophets.

While they were there, Jesus asked them a question concerning Psalm 110:1. Verses 41-46:

41 While the Pharisees were gathered together, Jesus asked them, 42 Saying, What think ye of Christ {Messiah]? whose son is he? They say unto him, The Son of David.

43 He saith unto them, How then doth David in spirit call him Lord, saying, 44 The LORD said unto my Lord, Sit thou on my right hand, till I make thine enemies thy footstool?

45 If David then call him Lord, how is he his son? 46 And no man was able to answer him a word, neither durst [dared] any man from that day forth ask him any more questions.

25

Matthew 23

Jesus first entered Jerusalem on what many call Palm Sunday. There were only four days between that day and the fateful Friday. It is during this time that Jesus continued to teach many people throughout Jerusalem. Matthew 23:1-3:

> 1 **Then spake Jesus to the multitude, and to his disciples, 2 Saying, The scribes and the Pharisees sit in Moses' seat:**
>
> 3 **All therefore whatsoever they bid you observe, that observe and do; but do not ye after their works: for they say, and do not.**

Jesus just told the people to do what these religious leaders tell you to do, but do not follow their example. He continues with verses 4-12:

4 For they bind heavy burdens and grievous to be borne, and lay them on men's shoulders; but they themselves will not move them with one of their fingers.

5 But all their works they do for to be seen of men: they make broad their phylacteries, and enlarge the borders of their garments,

6 And love the uppermost rooms at feasts, and the chief seats in the synagogues, 7 And greetings in the markets, and to be called of [by] men, Rabbi, Rabbi. 8 But be not ye called Rabbi: for [only] one is your Master, even [that is to say] Christ; and all ye are brethren.

9 And call no man your father upon the earth: for [only] one is your Father, which is in heaven. 10 Neither be ye called masters: for one is your Master, even [that is to say] Christ.

11 But he that is greatest among you shall be your servant. 12 And whosoever shall exalt himself shall be abased; and he that shall humble himself shall be

exalted.

Like many religions, the leaders are self-centric. They seek to expand the size and control of their own kingdom and they desire money and control. Jesus had knocked the hornets' nest down, and now he was kicking it.

As God's spokesperson, Jesus is speaking on God's behalf when He brings indictments against them. The word "woe" means "a condition of deep suffering, affliction, or grief." Verses 13-33:

13 **But woe unto you, scribes and Pharisees, [you] hypocrites! for ye shut up the kingdom of heaven against men: for ye neither go in yourselves, neither suffer [allow] ye them that are entering to go in.**

14 **Woe unto you, scribes and Pharisees, hypocrites! for ye devour widows' houses, and for a pretence make long prayer: therefore ye shall receive the greater damnation.**

15 **Woe unto you, scribes and Pharisees, hypocrites! for ye compass sea and land to make one proselyte, and when he is**

made, ye make him twofold more the child of hell than yourselves.

16 Woe unto you, ye blind guides, which say, Whosoever shall swear by the temple, it is nothing; but whosoever shall swear by the gold of the temple, he is a debtor! 17 Ye fools and blind: for whether is greater, the gold, or the temple that sanctifieth the gold?

18 And, [ye say] Whosoever shall swear by the altar, it is nothing; but whosoever sweareth by the gift that is upon it, he is guilty. 19 Ye fools and blind: for whether is greater, the gift, or the altar that sanctifieth the gift? 20 Whoso therefore shall swear by the altar, sweareth by it, and by all things thereon.

21 And whoso shall swear by the temple, sweareth by it, and by him that dwelleth therein. 22 And he that shall swear by heaven, sweareth by the throne of God, and by him that sitteth thereon.

23 Woe unto you, scribes and Pharisees, hypocrites! for ye pay tithe of mint and

anise and cummin, and have omitted the weightier matters of the law, judgment, mercy, and faith: these ought [should] ye to have done, and not to leave the other undone. 24 Ye blind guides, which strain at [out] a gnat, and swallow a camel.

25 Woe unto you, scribes and Pharisees, hypocrites! for ye make clean the outside of the cup and of the platter, but within they are full of extortion and excess. 26 Thou blind Pharisee, cleanse first that which is within the cup and platter, that the outside of them may be clean also.

27 Woe unto you, scribes and Pharisees, hypocrites! for ye are like unto whited [white-washed] sepulchres, which indeed appear beautiful outward, but are within full of dead men's bones, and of all uncleanness. 28 Even so ye also outwardly appear righteous unto men, but within ye are full of hypocrisy and iniquity.

29 Woe unto you, scribes and Pharisees, hypocrites! because ye build the tombs

of the prophets, and garnish the sepulchres of the righteous, 30 <u>And say, If we had been in the days of our fathers, we would not have been partakers with them in the blood of the prophets.</u>

31 <u>Wherefore ye be witnesses unto [against] yourselves, that ye are the children of them which killed the prophets.</u> 32 Fill ye up then the measure of your fathers. 33 Ye serpents, ye generation of vipers, how can ye escape the damnation of hell?

They said that if it had been them during the time of their fathers, then they would not have killed the prophets. Yet, just days away, they will kill their Messiah, the Son of God. They testify against themselves! Verses 34-36:

34 Wherefore, behold, I send unto you prophets, and wise men, and scribes: and some of them ye shall kill and crucify; and some of them shall ye scourge in your synagogues, and persecute them from city to city:

35 That upon you may come all the righteous blood shed upon the earth, from

the blood of righteous Abel unto the blood of Zacharias son of Barachias, whom ye slew between the temple and the altar.

36 Verily I say unto you, All these things shall come upon this generation.

Jesus mourns over Jerusalem, God's Holy City. Continually, Israel rejected God by rejecting His prophets. As in the story of the vineyard and the landowner, "But last of all he sent unto them his son, saying, They will reverence my son. But when the husbandmen saw the son, they said among themselves, This is the heir; come, let us kill him, and let us seize on his inheritance" (Matt. 21:37-38). Soon, like the husbandmen of the vineyard, they will kill God's Son. Verses 37-39:

37 O Jerusalem, Jerusalem, thou that killest the prophets, and stonest them which are sent unto thee, how often would I have gathered thy children together, even as a hen gathereth her chickens under her wings, and ye would not!

38 Behold, your house is left unto you desolate. **39** For I say unto you, Ye shall

201

not see me henceforth, till ye shall say, Blessed is he that cometh in the name of the Lord.

At a point in the future, the believing remnant of Israel will be in such a dire state that they will cry out to God. The LORD will intercede on their behalf and return to save them. But, not until Israel says, "Blessed is He that cometh in the name of the Lord!"

26

Matthew 24 (Part I)

When Jesus finished speaking, He and the disciples left the Temple. I picture that it was later in the day. As the sun set, a golden hue would envelop the Temple. His disciples stood momentarily in admiration and shared their thoughts with Jesus. Matthew 24:1-2:

> 1 **And Jesus went out, and departed from the temple: and his disciples came to him for to shew [show] him the buildings of the temple.**
>
> 2 **And Jesus said unto them, See ye not all these things? verily I say unto you, There shall not be left here one stone upon another, that shall not be thrown down.**

Jesus speaks not only about Jerusalem's future, but of the future of Israel and Judah. This brought about the following discussion. Before we continue, there are some points I would like to make. Jesus is speaking to His disciples who are Jewish. His answer is directed to them. It concerns a point in time when the Kingdom will be established. Jesus' response involves the coming Tribulation which is also known as "Jacob's Time of Trouble." Jeremiah 30:4-9:

> 4 **And these are the words that the LORD spake <u>concerning Israel and concerning Judah</u>. 5 For thus saith the LORD; We have heard <u>a voice of trembling, of fear, and not of peace</u>.**
>
> 6 **Ask ye now, and see whether a man doth travail with child? wherefore do I see every man with his hands on his loins, as a woman in travail, and <u>all faces are turned into paleness</u>?**
>
> 7 <u>**Alas! for that day is great, so that none is like it: it is even the time of Jacob's trouble; but he shall be saved out of it.**</u>
>
> 8 **For it shall come to pass in that day, saith the LORD of hosts, that I will break his yoke from off thy neck, and**

will burst thy bonds, and strangers shall no more serve themselves of him:

⁹ But <u>they shall serve the LORD their God, and David their king, whom I will raise up unto them.</u>

Most importantly, all of this falls perfectly within the timeline established in Daniel 9. We must keep in mind to whom Jesus is speaking. Here are their questions and Jesus' answers. Matthew 24:3-8:

3 And as he sat upon the mount of Olives, the disciples came unto him privately, saying, <u>Tell us, when shall these things be? and what shall be the sign of thy coming, and of the end of the world?</u>

4 And Jesus answered and said unto them, Take heed that no man deceive you. 5 For many shall come in my name, saying, I am Christ; and shall deceive many.

6 And ye shall hear of wars and rumours of wars: see that ye be not troubled: for all these things must come to pass, but

the end is not yet. 7 For nation shall rise against nation, and kingdom against kingdom: and there shall be famines, and pestilences, and earthquakes, in divers [different] places. 8 <u>All these are the beginning of sorrows.</u>

During the Tribulation, those who follow the Gospel of the Kingdom will be tortured and killed. Violence and lawlessness will be commonplace. Verses 9-13:

9 Then shall they deliver you up to be afflicted, and shall kill you: and ye shall be hated of [by] all nations for my name's sake.

10 And then shall many be offended, and shall betray one another, and shall hate one another. 11 And many false prophets shall rise, and shall deceive many.

12 And because iniquity shall abound, the love of many shall wax [grow] cold. 13 <u>But he that shall endure unto the end, the same shall be saved.</u>

Here is the proof of what was stated previously.

Those who believe the Gospel of the Kingdom must continually prove their faith by good works. Furthermore, they must "endure unto the end." Only then, will they receive their salvation when the Messiah returns to establish His Kingdom.

Those believers who follow the Gospel of Grace preached by the Apostle Paul are following a different gospel. (See Galatians 2:6-9.) Matthew 24 is dealing with three things: the Jews, their unique gospel, and the future Kingdom promised to King David. Now, let us return to Matthew 24:14:

> 14 And this **gospel of the kingdom shall be preached in all the world for a witness unto all nations;** and then shall the end come.

Here, we must stop again. We know that the seven-year Tribulation or "Jacob's Time of Trouble" is coming. We learned something important from the last verse. During these last seven years that precede the end, the Gospel of the Kingdom will be preached; not the Gospel of Grace! When Jesus answers His disciples, He refers to a prophecy that was very familiar to the Jews at that time. He offers no explanation, but simply makes statements which they understand.

However, for you, an explanation is needed.

Jesus is answering the question asked by the disciples, "Tell us, when shall these things be? and what shall be the sign of thy coming, and of the end of the world?" (v. 3). He begins by referring to the prophecy of the coming Kingdom in Daniel 9. In his prayer, Daniel asked God when He would restore His City, Jerusalem. It was destroyed by the Babylonians when King Nebuchadnezzar took the Jews captive and brought them to Babylon. God sent them into exile for seventy years as punishment for breaking His covenant. God heard Daniel's prayer but His reply gave him something far greater. He gave him a biblical timeline. The answer Daniel received went far beyond the physical restoration of Jerusalem. Instead, it dealt with the future New Jerusalem that comes down from heaven after the Tribulation. (See Revelation 21:2.)

Since understanding this timeline is crucial to understanding what Jesus is telling His disciples, we need to stop. We must focus on this prophecy before we continue. This will allow us to place these events within Daniel's timeline. The following is an excerpt from my book *The Hidden Gospel* which summarizes Daniel's prophecy.

"Jerusalem would be restored as God's Holy City. It would become home to His eternal Kingdom ruled by the eternal King! Let's break down Daniel's prophecy into bite-size pieces. The brackets are added for clarification. Daniel 9:24:

> 24 **Seventy weeks are determined upon thy people and upon thy holy city, to [1] finish the transgression, and [2] to make an end of sins, and [3] to make reconciliation for iniquity, and [4] to bring in everlasting righteousness, and [5] to seal up the vision and prophecy, and [6] to anoint the most Holy.**

"Daniel was told that, at the end of this seventy weeks, God will accomplish the six items numbered above. These will complete God's plan to restore His Creation. God will: (1) end sin, (2) make payment for sin, (3) reconcile creation to Himself, (4) establish everlasting righteousness, (5) fulfill the promises and prophecies, and (6) anoint the most Holy One. This is the Lord Jesus Christ, the King of kings and Lord of lords. God's ultimate plan for complete restoration of Creation will be complete!

"There is something that I need to clarify before we go on. In this prophecy, each day of the week represents one year. Therefore, one week would be seven years. Seventy weeks would be 490 years. This is a valuable timeline for understanding the end times. Later on, you may want to consider additional reading. I recommend Sir Robert Anderson's *The Coming Prince: The Marvelous Prophecy of Daniel's Seventy Weeks Concerning the Antichrist.* Both *Letters To Theophilus* and *The Glorious Destiny of Israel* are excellent as well.

"Now, let us continue with the prophecy. The angel is going to break it down for us. This will be very interesting as it explains so much. Verse 25:

> 25 **Know therefore and understand, that from the going forth of the commandment to restore and to build Jerusalem unto the Messiah the Prince shall be <u>seven weeks, and threescore and two weeks</u>: the street shall be built again, and the wall, even in troublous times.**

"Let us do some simple addition. Add seven plus three score which is sixty. Then, add two. The sum is sixty-nine weeks. Then, multiply sixty-nine by seven. We get 483 years. The next verse restates it, but do not forget to include the seven years from verse 25 to equal the sixty-nine weeks. Verse 26:

26 [1] And after threescore and two

weeks <u>shall Messiah be cut off</u>, but not for himself: and [2] <u>the people of the prince that shall come shall destroy the city</u> and the sanctuary; and the end thereof shall be with a flood [of people], and unto the end of the war desolations are determined.

"Archaeologists have dated the command "to restore and to build Jerusalem" to 453 BC. If we subtract 483 years, then we get a negative thirty. The difference would be the date of 30 AD when the Messiah was cut off. The words "the people of the prince" are followers of the prince or the Antichrist. The angel speaks about a "flood" which is a "flood of people" so numerous that they appear as water. This is the remaining seven years and it will continue "unto the end." (See Matthew 24.)

"This prince will make a covenant or agreement with many nations at the beginning of the seven years. Verse 27:

27 And he [the prince] shall confirm the covenant with many for one week [seven years]: and in the midst of the week he shall cause the sacrifice and the oblation [non-blood offerings] to cease, and for the overspreading of abomina-

tions he shall make it desolate, even until the consummation [the completion or end], and that [which is] determined shall be poured upon the desolate.

"In the middle of these seven years, the Antichrist will break the covenant he made. In Revelation, this midpoint is referred to as three and one-half years, forty-two months, or 1,260 days. They are the same. From the midpoint, the remaining time that following will be considered the Great Tribulation. Consider the words of Jesus Christ concerning this time. Matthew 24:22:

22 **And except those days should be shortened, there should no flesh be saved: but for the elect's [Israel's] sake those days shall be shortened.**

"The reply Daniel received from God answered far more than his question. He asked God when He would restore fallen Jerusalem and, now, we have a timeline. This timeline began at the decree "to restore and to build Jerusalem" which has been accurately dated to 453 BC. We know that 483 years into this timeline, the Messiah will be cut off for a while. If we add 483 years to 453 BC, we come to 30 AD. Interesting! This would date the crucifixion to 30 AD. It was forty years after His crucifixion that the City of Jerusalem was destroyed in 70 AD. So, what happened?

"The timeline began some 2500 years ago. This prophecy should have been fulfilled a long time ago. God knew the Jews would reject their Messiah. However, He did not change the timeline. Nothing changed. The seven remaining years are currently being held in abeyance – in temporary suspension."[1]

In the next chapter of this book, we will continue with the remainder of Matthew 24.

---

[1] Greene, David Alan. The Hidden Gospel: Once Hidden But Now Revealed. 2nd Edition. (USA: GraceWord Publishing, 2024), 64-68.

27

Matthew 24 (Part II)

The disciples listened to Jesus answer their question, "Tell us, when shall these things be? and what shall be the sign of thy coming, and of the end of the world?" (v. 3). Jesus is speaking about the mid-point of the seven years. Matthew 24:15-17:

> 15 **When ye therefore shall see the abomination of desolation, spoken of by Daniel the prophet, stand in the holy place, (whoso readeth, let him understand:)**

> 16 **Then let them which be in Judaea flee into the mountains: 17 Let him which is on the housetop not come down to take any thing out of his house:**

The prince is the antichrist. When He appears, the

Jews are to leave Jerusalem at once as this marks the middle of the seven years. For those unfamiliar with the end times, the Rapture precedes the appearance of the Antichrist and the beginning of the Tribulation.

Jesus continues in verses 18-21:

18 **Neither let him which is in the field return back to take his clothes.** 19 **And woe unto them that are with child, and to them that give suck [nurse] in those days!**

20 **But pray ye that your flight be not in the winter, neither on the sabbath day:**

21 **For then shall be <u>great tribulation</u>, such as was not since the beginning of the world to this time, no, nor ever shall be.**

The great tribulation begins at the mid-point. This is when the Antichrist enters the Temple and proclaims himself to be god. Verse 22:

22 **And except those days should be shortened, there should no flesh be saved: but for the elect's sake those days**

216

shall be shortened.

Concerning these last three and one-half years, Jesus said, "except those days should be shortened, there should no flesh be saved" (v. 22). This is how dire the situation will be for all mankind.

During this time, there will be many false teachers to confuse and lead people astray. I once had a Baptist minister tell me that he did not want to be raptured. He wanted to stay and keep proclaiming the gospel. Although he had become aware of the two gospels explained above, I looked at him and asked him, "Which one?" Remember, following the Rapture, the Gospel of Grace will no longer be offered. The only choice will be, as Jesus stated above, the Gospel of the Kingdom. Verses 23-28:

> **23 Then if any man shall say unto you, Lo, here is Christ, or there; believe it not. 24 For there shall arise false Christs, and false prophets, and shall shew great signs and wonders; insomuch that, if it were possible, they shall deceive the very elect.**

> **25 Behold, I have told you before. 26 Wherefore if they shall say unto you, Behold, he is in the desert; go not forth:**

behold, he is in the secret chambers; believe it not.

27 For as the lightning cometh out of the
east, and shineth even unto the west; so
shall also the coming of the Son of man
be. 28 For wheresoever the carcase [dead
body] is, there will the eagles be gathered together.

The book of Revelation goes into details of the
Tribulation. We know at the end there is a great battle called the Battle of Armageddon. At that point,
the Messiah will return as King to save Israel and destroy their enemies. Now, Jesus is speaking about the
end of the Tribulation and His appearing as the Son
of Man. Verses 29-30:

29 Immediately after [at the close of] the
tribulation of those days shall the sun
be darkened, and the moon shall not
give her light, and the stars shall fall
from heaven, and the powers of the
heavens shall be shaken:

30 And then shall appear the sign of the
Son of man in heaven: and then shall all
the tribes of the earth mourn, and they
shall see the Son of man coming in the

clouds of heaven with power and great glory.

Above, the words "the tribes of the earth" refer to the Gentile nations. At the Tower of Babel, God created all the nations. From this group, God called one man, Abraham, from among these nations to create the nation of Israel.

The trumpet will announce the arrival of the Son of Man. It will be quite glorious and frightening: glorious for Israel and frightening for the nations who sought to destroy her. God will gather scattered Israel from every corner of Creation. Verse 31:

> 31 **And he shall send his angels with a great sound of a trumpet, and they shall gather together his elect from the four winds, from one end of heaven to the other.**

Do you recall the words Jesus spoke when He entered Jerusalem? Matthew 23:37:

> 37 **O Jerusalem, Jerusalem, thou that killest the prophets, and stonest them which are sent unto thee, how often would I have gathered thy children together, even as a hen gathereth her**

chickens under her wings, and ye would not!

Jesus reminds His disciples of the parable of the fig tree. (See Matt. 21:18-21.) In it, Jesus cursed the barren fig tree for failing to produce fruit. He was figuratively speaking about unbelieving Israel. Matthew 24:32-35:

32 **Now learn a parable of the fig tree; When his branch is yet tender, and putteth forth leaves, ye know that summer is nigh [near]:**

33 <u>**So likewise ye, when ye shall see all these things, know that it is near, even at the doors.**</u> 34 <u>**Verily I say unto you, This generation shall not pass, till all these things be fulfilled.**</u>

35 **Heaven and earth shall pass away, but my words shall not pass away.**

As Jesus was telling His Disciple this, the Tribulation was imminent. Daniel's 490-year prophecy would be fulfilled in just seven years. However, we find in the latter portion of the book of Acts, there is a temporary suspension of Daniel's timeline. Certainly, something has happened. At the time of writing this book, we have almost reached the 2000th anniversary of Jesus' death, burial, and resurrection.

Jesus compares this with the last cataclysmic judgment upon the entire earth by water. Noah preached repentance for 120 years before that judgment. Then, the door to the Ark was shut and the rain began. The opportunity for salvation was removed. I like to tell the story of those who were outside the safety of the Ark. As the rains fell, the sound of people beating upon the hull could be heard until there was only the sound of the wind and the rain. It is this ominous thought of destruction that Jesus wishes to convey. Until that judgment, it was just an ordinary day. Verses 36-39:

> 36 **But of that day and hour knoweth no man, no, not the angels of heaven, but my Father only.**
>
> 37 **But as the days of Noe were, so shall also the coming of the Son of man be.** 38 **For as in the days that were before the flood they were eating and drinking, marrying and giving in marriage, until the day that Noe entered into the ark,** 39 **And knew not until the flood came, and took them all away; so shall also the coming of the Son of man be.**

The following verse is misunderstood by many. However, if we see it correctly it will make sense. We are talking about the Age of Law; not the Age of Grace. Jesus is speaking about the time that follows the Rapture. So, the Age of Grace ended. He is now speaking about establishing the earthly Kingdom. Like the sifting of wheat, there are those that remain who believe while others do not. The following verse refers to them. Verse 40-41:

> 40 **Then shall two be in the field; the one shall be taken [away], and the other left.** 41 **Two women shall be grinding at the mill; the one shall be taken [away], and the other left.**

Faithful Israel and the Gentiles who blessed them will remain on earth. Israel's inheritance is earthly! They will receive the New Jerusalem! Something that all faithful Jews desire. The Apostle John was an eyewitness of the future. He confirms it in Revelation 21:1-2:

> 1 **And I saw a new heaven and a new earth: for the first heaven and the first earth were passed away; and there was no more sea.** 2 **And I John saw the holy city, new Jerusalem, coming down from**

God out of heaven, prepared as a bride adorned for her husband.

I wrote a book devoted to the glorious destiny of God's people. All the promises and prophecies that God made to Israel will be, repeat, will be fulfilled. The book is titled *The Glorious Destiny of Israel*. Since it is dedicated exclusively to Israel, it does not discuss God's offer of salvation by grace. That is discussed in another book titled *Letters To Theophilus*.

The children of Abraham must be prepared. God will do what He said He will do. They must continually watch and be ready. Matthew 24:42-44:

> 42 **Watch therefore: for ye know not what hour your Lord doth come.**
>
> 43 **But know this, that if the goodman of the house had known in what watch the thief would come, he would have watched, and would not have suffered [allowed] his house to be broken up.**
>
> 44 **Therefore be ye also ready: for in such an hour as ye think not the Son of man cometh.**

He continues by speaking about those whose Master returns to find them doing what is expected of them. Verses 45-47:

> 45 Who then is a faithful and wise serv-
> ant, whom his lord hath made ruler over
> his household, to give them meat in due
> season?
>
> 46 Blessed is that servant, whom his lord
> when he cometh shall find so doing. 47
> Verily I say unto you, That he shall
> make him ruler over all his goods.

For those who do not do what is expected of them, there will be consequences. Verses 48-51:

> 48 But and if that evil servant shall say
> in his heart, My lord delayeth his com-
> ing; 49 And shall begin to smite his fel-
> lowservants, and to eat and drink with
> the drunken;
>
> 50 The lord of that servant shall come in
> a day when he looketh not for him, and
> in an hour that he is not aware of, 51 And
> shall cut him asunder, and appoint him
> his portion with the hypocrites: there
> shall be weeping and gnashing of teeth.

28

Matthew 25

Jesus returns to publicly teaching about the Kingdom of Heaven. The capital of this eternal Kingdom is Jerusalem. However, the current city of Jerusalem will be replaced with a new one. In Revelation, the Apostle John goes into great detail about the New Jerusalem. We mentioned earlier that it descends out of heaven like a bride on her wedding day. John begins his description with Revelation 21:10:

> 10 **And he carried me away in the spirit to a great and high mountain, and shewed me that great city, the holy Jerusalem, descending out of heaven from God,**

Surprisingly, there is no Temple in the New Jerusalem. John explains the reason for this in Revelation 21:22:

22 And I saw no temple therein: for the Lord God Almighty and the Lamb are the temple of it.

So, the capital city of the earthly Kingdom, currently being prepared for Israel, is in heaven.

With this in mind, let us go to our text. Matthew 25:1-13:

1 Then shall the kingdom of heaven be likened unto ten virgins, which took their lamps, and went forth to meet the bridegroom.

2 And five of them were wise, and five were foolish. **3** They that were foolish took their lamps, and took no oil with them: **4** But the wise took oil in their vessels with their lamps. **5** While the bridegroom tarried, they all slumbered and slept.

6 And at midnight there was a cry made, Behold, the bridegroom cometh; go ye out to meet him. **7** Then all those virgins arose, and trimmed their lamps. **8** And the foolish said unto the wise, Give us of [from] your oil; for our lamps are gone out. 9 But the wise answered, saying, Not so; lest there be not enough for us and you: but go ye rather to them that sell, and buy for yourselves.

10 And while they went to buy, the bridegroom came; and they that were ready went in with him to the marriage: and the door was shut. 11 Afterward came also the other virgins, saying, Lord, Lord, open to us. 12 But he answered and said, Verily I say unto you, I know you not.

13 Watch therefore, for ye know neither the day nor the hour wherein the Son of man cometh.

The above warns of the need for both expectation and preparedness for all Kingdom Believers. How are they to do this? They are to keep the Law. They are to keep the faith and provide fruit or proof of that faith by good works.

Jesus uses another comparison in the following parable. Each believer is expected to use the talents or skills given to them. They are to be used by them for the benefit of the Giver. Verses 14-30:

14 For the kingdom of heaven is as a man travelling into a far country, who called his own servants, and delivered unto them his goods.

15 And unto one he gave five talents, to another two, and to another one; to every man according to his several [individual] ability; and straightway took his journey.

16 Then he that had received the five talents went and traded with the same, and made them other five talents. 17 And likewise he that had received two, he also gained other two. 18 But he that had received one went and digged in the earth, and hid his lord's money.

19 After a long time the lord of those servants cometh, and reckoneth with them.

20 And so he that had received five talents came and brought other five talents, saying, Lord, thou deliveredst unto me five talents: behold, I have gained beside them five talents more.

21 His lord said unto him, Well done, thou good and faithful servant: thou hast been faithful over a few things, I will make thee ruler over many things: enter thou into the joy of thy lord.

22 He also that had received two talents came and said, Lord, thou deliveredst unto me two talents: behold, I have gained two other talents beside them.

23 His lord said unto him, Well done, good and faithful servant; thou hast been faithful over a few things, I will make thee ruler over many things: enter thou into the joy of thy lord.

24 Then he which had received the one talent came and said, Lord, I knew thee that thou art an hard man, reaping where thou hast not sown, and gathering where thou hast not strawed: 25 And I was afraid, and went and hid thy talent in the earth: lo, there thou hast that is thine.

26 His lord answered and said unto him, Thou wicked and slothful servant, thou knewest that I reap where I sowed not,

and gather where I have not strawed: 27 **Thou oughtest therefore to have put my money to the exchangers, and then at my coming I should have received mine own with usury [interest].** 28 **Take therefore the talent from him, and give it unto him which hath ten talents.**

29 **For unto every one that hath shall be given, and he shall have abundance: but from him that hath not shall be taken away even that which he hath.** 30 **And cast ye the unprofitable servant into outer darkness: there shall be weeping and gnashing of teeth.**

In the above parable, the investments made by each individual and returns given to their Master are to be viewed within the context of the Kingdom. This is not to be seen from a worldly prospective. Here, the Master was not looking for material gain, but rather a spiritual gain. The Jews, like a tree, must continually produce fruit. As in the example of the fig tree, they are to bring forth their expected harvest. One brought forth a fruitful bounty, one a marginal bounty, and the last brought forth nothing. And, as with the example of the fig tree that bore no fruit, he was cursed. The measure of talents or skills are a blessing. As such, the Giver of gifts expects a return.

The following refers to the return of the Messiah. It is called the Second Coming. Like the closing of the door of Noah's Ark and the closing of the Age of Grace with the Rapture, the Tribulation will come to a close with the arrival of the King of Kings. Until then, the faithful Jews who keep the Law, keep their faith, and endured unto the end, will receive their salvation. Verses 31-34:

> 31 When the Son of man shall come in his glory, and all the holy angels with him, then shall he sit upon the throne of his glory: 32 And before him shall be gathered all nations: and he shall separate them one from another, as a shepherd divideth his sheep from the goats:
>
> 33 And he shall set the sheep on his right hand, but the goats on the left. 34 Then shall the King say unto them on his right hand, Come, ye blessed of my Father, inherit the kingdom prepared for you from the foundation of the world:

How then will He judge their works or faith? He shall determine it by the love they showed to others because they loved God. Verses 35-40:

> 35 For I was an hungred, and ye gave me

meat: I was thirsty, and ye gave me drink: I was a stranger, and ye took me in: 36 Naked, and ye clothed me: I was sick, and ye visited me: I was in prison, and ye came unto me.

37 Then shall the righteous answer him, saying, Lord, when saw we thee an hungred, and fed thee? or thirsty, and gave thee drink? 38 When saw we thee a stranger, and took thee in? or naked, and clothed thee? 39 Or when saw we thee sick, or in prison, and came unto thee?

40 And the King shall answer and say unto them, Verily I say unto you, Inasmuch as ye have done it unto one of the least of these my brethren, ye have done it unto me.

When the Jews showed love to their brethren, they were showing the love and faith they had in God. And, for this, they will be rewarded.

However, there are those who did not show any compassion or love to others. They were miserly with their love and, like the fig tree, bore no fruit of love toward their brethren. Verses 41-46:

41 Then shall he say also unto them on the left hand, Depart from me, ye cursed, into everlasting fire, prepared for the devil and his angels:

42 For I was an hungred, and ye gave me no meat: I was thirsty, and ye gave me no drink: 43 I was a stranger, and ye took me not in: naked, and ye clothed me not: sick, and in prison, and ye visited me not.

44 Then shall they also answer him, saying, Lord, when saw we thee an hungred, or athirst, or a stranger, or naked, or sick, or in prison, and did not minister unto thee?

45 Then shall he answer them, saying, Verily I say unto you, Inasmuch as ye did it not to one of the least of these, ye did it not to me.

46 And these shall go away into everlasting punishment: but the righteous into life eternal.

29

Matthew 26 (Part I)

Jesus wanted to tell His disciples what would happen to Him. He did not want them to be unaware. Later in the narrative, we will see that, although they heard Jesus's words, they did not understand them. Matthew 26:1-2:

> 1 **And it came to pass, when Jesus had finished all these sayings, he said unto his disciples, 2 Ye know that after two days is the feast of the passover, and the Son of man is betrayed to be crucified.**

As He spoke, plans were being made by the religious leaders against Him. Verses 3-5:

> 3 **Then assembled together the chief priests, and the scribes, and the elders of the people, unto the palace of the**

high priest, who was called Caiaphas, 4 And consulted that they might take Jesus by subtilty, and kill him.

5 But they said, Not on the feast day, lest there be an uproar among the people.

Jesus continues His ministry to the lost sheep of Israel. Verses 6-13:

6 Now when Jesus was in Bethany, in the house of Simon the leper, 7 There came unto him a woman having an alabaster box of very precious ointment, and poured it on his head, as he sat at meat [a meal].

8 But when his disciples saw it, they had indignation, saying, To what purpose is this waste? 9 For this ointment might have been sold for much, and given to the poor.

10 When Jesus understood it, he said unto them, Why trouble ye the woman? for she hath wrought [done] a good work upon me.

11 For ye have the poor always with

you; but me ye have not always. 12 For in that she hath poured this ointment on my body, she did it for my burial.

13 Verily I say unto you, Wheresoever this gospel shall be preached in the whole world, there shall also this, that [what] this woman hath done, be told for a memorial of her.

What this woman did with this fine ointment was to prepare Jesus' body for His imminent burial.

There has been much discussion as to why Judas betrayed the Son of Man. He chose to do this, but why? Some supposed that it was to force Jesus into action. The Zealots wanted the Messiah to destroy their enemies and break the yoke of bondage under the Romans. Either way, Judas was paid by the religious leaders to betray Jesus. Verses 14-16:

14 Then one of the twelve, called Judas Iscariot, went unto the chief priests,

15 And said unto them, What will ye give me, and I will deliver him unto you? And they covenanted [agreed] with him for thirty pieces of silver.

**16 And from that time he sought oppor-
tunity to betray him.**

The Passover feast is celebrated annually as a
memorial of an historic event: the night the Angel of
Death went throughout Egypt taking the life of every
first born. Pharoah had rejected Moses' request to,
"Let my people go." Moses told Pharoah that this
judgment would come upon the House of Pharoah
and all Egypt. The Jews were instructed to mark their
doorways with the blood of a sacrificed lamb and the
Angel of Death would "pass over" their household.
For that reason, John the Baptist said of Jesus, "Behold the Lamb of God!" (Jn. 1:36). It is for this feast
that the disciples prepare. Verses 17-25:

**17 Now the first day of the feast of un-
leavened bread the disciples came to Jesus, saying unto him, Where wilt thou
that we prepare for thee to eat the passover?**

**18 And he said, Go into the city to such
a man, and say unto him, The Master
saith, My time is at hand; I will keep the
passover at thy house with my disciples. 19 And the disciples did as Jesus
had appointed them; and they made
ready the passover.**

20 Now when the even [evening] was come, he sat down with the twelve. 21 And as they did eat, he said, Verily I say unto you, that one of you shall betray me. 22 And they were exceeding sorrowful, and began every one of them to say unto him, Lord, is it I? 23 And he answered and said, He that dippeth his hand with me in the dish, the same shall betray me.

24 The Son of man goeth as it is written of him: but woe unto that man by whom the Son of man is betrayed! it had been good [better] for that man if he had not been born. 25 Then Judas, which betrayed him, answered and said, Master, is it I? He said unto him, Thou hast said.

Now, in this Passover meal, they are sharing in what will later become communion. Verses 26-27:

26 And as they were eating, Jesus took bread, and blessed it, and brake it, and gave it to the disciples, and said, <u>Take, eat; this is my body.</u> 27 And he took the cup, and gave thanks, and gave it to them, saying, Drink ye all of it;

Jesus explains to them its significance. Verses 28-30:

> **28 <u>For this is my blood of the new testa-</u><u>ment</u>, which is shed for many for the re-mission of sins.**

> **29 But I say unto you<u>, I will not drink</u><u>henceforth of this fruit of the vine, until</u><u>that day when I drink it new with you</u><u>in my Father's kingdom.</u> 30 And when they had sung an hymn, they went out into the mount of Olives.**

We will pause here as there is something I want you to see what few people do. Did you notice Jesus gave no explanation at the meal about this New Testament or covenant? It is because the disciples understood the reference He was making to the prophecy given by Jeremiah. We need to look at that prophecy and apply it to the present context.

Throughout the Old Testament, we read about Israel's constant failures to keep God's Law and their faith in His Word. God knew this, but promises had been made and God Himself intended to fulfill those promises regardless of Israel's failures. Jeremiah 31:31-32:

> **31 Behold, the days come, saith the**

LORD, that <u>I will make a new covenant with the house of Israel, and with the house of Judah</u>:

32 <u>Not according to the covenant that I made with their fathers in the day that I took them by the hand to bring them out of the land of Egypt;</u> which my covenant they brake, although I was an husband unto them, saith the LORD:

This New Covenant is referred to above by Jesus as the New Testament. Jeremiah continues. Verse 33:

33 But this shall be the covenant that I will make with the house of Israel; After those days, saith the LORD, <u>I will put my law in their inward parts, and write it in their hearts; and will be their God, and they shall be my people</u>.

God intends on fulfilling righteousness on behalf of Israel through His Son. This will only apply to those who accept Him as their Messiah and the Son of God. They must follow the Law of Moses and He will intercede for them. If they keep the covenant, then they will receive their salvation when He returns to establish His Kingdom. We see the fulfillment of this in Revelation.

Jesus continues to tell the disciples what will happen in the near future. Before you continue, please stop for a moment and read Zechariah 13:7-9 which is referred to below. Matthew 26:31-32:

> 31 Then saith Jesus unto them, All ye shall be offended because of me this night: for it is written, I will smite the shepherd, and the sheep of the flock shall be scattered abroad.
>
> 32 But after I am risen again, I will go before you into Galilee.

Peter was always the outspoken one of the group. He swears allegiance to Jesus, but Jesus responds with a prophecy. Verses 33-35:

> 33 Peter answered and said unto him, Though all men shall be offended because of thee, yet will I never be offended.
>
> 34 Jesus said unto him, Verily I say unto thee, That this night, before the cock crow, thou shalt deny me thrice. 35 Peter said unto him, Though I should die with thee, yet will I not deny thee. Likewise also said all the disciples.

30

Matthew 26 (Part II)

We find in the Gospel of John that Judas left after taking communion with the others. (See John 13:26-27.) This would make a good argument that believers are not saved by communion even if they took communion with the Lord Jesus Christ Himself. It was evening; morning would come soon. They went to the Garden of Gethsemane where Jesus desired to pray. His time was drawing to its conclusion and He desired to be alone with the Father. Matthew 26:36-46:

> 36 Then cometh Jesus with them unto a place called Gethsemane, and saith unto the disciples, Sit ye here, while I go and pray yonder. 37 And he took with him Peter and the two sons of Zebedee, and began to be sorrowful and very heavy.

38 Then saith he unto them, My soul is exceeding sorrowful, even unto death: tarry [wait] ye here, and watch with me.

39 And he went a little further, and fell on his face, and prayed, saying, O my Father, if it be possible, let this cup pass from me: nevertheless not as I will, but as thou wilt.

40 And he cometh unto the disciples, and findeth them asleep, and saith unto Peter, What, could ye not watch with me one hour? 41 Watch and pray, that ye enter not into temptation: the spirit indeed is willing, but the flesh is weak.

42 He went away again the second time, and prayed, saying, O my Father, if this cup may not pass away from me, except I drink it, thy will be done.

43 And he came and found them asleep again: for their eyes were heavy. 44 And he left them, and went away again, and prayed the third time, saying the same words.

45 Then cometh he to his disciples, and

saith unto them, Sleep on now, and take your rest: behold, the hour is at hand, and the Son of man is betrayed into the hands of sinners.

46 Rise, let us be going: behold, he is at hand that doth betray me.

Judas brought the religious leaders and an armed crowd of their supporters to arrest Jesus. Verses 47-49:

47 And while he yet spake, lo, Judas, one of the twelve, came, and with him a great multitude with swords and staves, from the chief priests and elders of the people.

48 Now he that betrayed him gave them a sign, saying, Whomsoever I shall kiss, that same is he: hold him fast. 49 And forthwith he came to Jesus, and said, Hail, master; and kissed him.

In the heat of this confrontation, one of the Twelve would cut off an ear from a servant of the high priest. Although not mentioned here, in Luke's record, Jesus heals his ear. (See Luke 22:51.) Matthew records the dialog. Verses 50-54:

50 And Jesus said unto him, Friend, wherefore [why] art thou come? Then came they, and laid hands on Jesus, and took him.

51 And, behold, one of them which were with Jesus stretched out his hand, and drew his sword, and struck a servant of the high priest, and smote off his ear.

52 Then said Jesus unto him, Put up again thy sword into his place: for all they that take the sword shall perish with the sword. 53 Thinkest thou that I cannot now pray to my Father, and he shall presently give me more than twelve legions of angels?

54 But how then shall the scriptures be fulfilled, that thus it must be?

Jesus addresses the crowd that had come to his arrest. For those who are not familiar with how the name of God came to be, here it is. Exodus 3:13-15:

13 And Moses said unto God, Behold, when I come unto the children of Israel, and shall say unto them, The God of your fathers hath sent me unto you; and

they shall say to me, What is his name? what shall I say unto them?

14 And God said unto Moses, <u>I AM THAT I AM</u>: and he said, Thus shalt thou say unto the children of Israel, <u>I AM hath sent me unto you.</u>

15 And God said moreover unto Moses, Thus shalt thou say unto the children of Israel, The LORD God of your fathers, the God of Abraham, the God of Isaac, and the God of Jacob, hath sent me unto you: this is my name for ever, and this is my memorial unto all generations.

I tell you this because there is a part of this event that the Apostle John shares in his gospel. John 18:3-6:

3 Judas then, having received a band of men and officers from the chief priests and Pharisees, cometh thither with lanterns and torches and weapons.

4 Jesus therefore, knowing all things that should come upon him, went forth, and said unto them, Whom seek ye?

5 They answered him, Jesus of Naza-

reth. Jesus saith unto them, <u>I am</u> he. And Judas also, which betrayed him, stood with them.

6 <u>As soon then as he had said unto them, I am he, they [all] went backward, and fell to the ground.</u>

The name of God is a powerful name!

Let us continue with our text. Matthew 55-56:

55 **In that same hour said Jesus to the multitudes, Are ye come out as against a thief with swords and staves for to take me? I sat daily with you teaching in the temple, and ye laid no hold on me.**

56 **But all this was done, that the scriptures of the prophets might be fulfilled. Then all the disciples forsook him, and fled.**

Jesus was brought before His accuser, the chief priest by the name of Caiaphas. They found witnesses who would falsely testify against Him. Finally, they sentenced Him to death for blasphemy. Verses 57-68:

57 And they that had laid hold on Jesus led him away to Caiaphas the high priest, where the scribes and the elders were assembled.

58 But Peter followed him afar off unto the high priest's palace, and went in, and sat with the servants, to see the end.

59 Now the chief priests, and elders, and all the council, sought false witness against Jesus, to put him to death;

60 But found none: yea, though many false witnesses came, yet found they none. At the last came two false witnesses,

61 And said, This fellow said, I am able to destroy the temple of God, and to build it in three days.

62 And the high priest arose, and said unto him, Answerest thou nothing? what is it which these witness against thee? 63 But Jesus held his peace. And the high priest answered and said unto him, I adjure thee by the living God, that thou tell us whether thou be the

Christ, the Son of God.

64 Jesus saith unto him, Thou hast said: nevertheless I say unto you, Hereafter shall ye see the Son of man sitting on the right hand of power, and coming in the clouds of heaven.

65 Then the high priest rent [tore] his clothes, saying, He hath spoken blasphemy; what further need have we of witnesses? behold, now ye have heard his blasphemy.

66 What think ye? They answered and said, He is guilty of death.

67 Then did they spit in his face, and buffeted him; and others smote him with the palms of their hands, 68 Saying, Prophesy unto us, thou Christ, Who is he that smote thee?

In verse 56, we are told that all His disciples had scattered. So, Jesus was alone when He was brought before Caiaphas. However, Peter remained within close proximity to His Lord. Verses 69-75

69 Now Peter sat without in the palace:

and a damsel came unto him, saying, Thou also wast with Jesus of Galilee. 70 But he denied before them all, saying, I know not what thou sayest.

71 And when he was gone out into the porch, another maid saw him, and said unto them that were there, This fellow was also with Jesus of Nazareth. 72 And again he denied with an oath, I do not know the man.

73 And after a while came unto him they that stood by, and said to Peter, Surely thou also art one of them; for thy speech betrayeth thee.

74 Then began he to curse and to swear, saying, I know not the man. And immediately the cock crew. 75 And Peter remembered the word of Jesus, which said unto him, Before the cock crow, thou shalt deny me thrice. And he went out, and wept bitterly.

31

Matthew 27

The morning of His crucifixion, the religious leaders were planning what to do with Him. They came up with a plan to kill Him. However, it needed to be done by the Roman authorities in order to distance themselves. Matthew 27:1-2:

> 1 **When the morning was come, all the chief priests and elders of the people took counsel against Jesus to put him to death: 2 And when they had bound him, they led him away, and delivered him to Pontius Pilate the governor.**

Jesus was condemned to death. This was not what Judas expected. He repented, or changed his mind, and went back to the religious leaders. Having achieved their objective, their response to Judas was, "What is that to us?" Verses 3-10:

3 Then Judas, which had betrayed him, when he saw that he was condemned, repented himself, and brought again the thirty pieces of silver to the chief priests and elders, 4 Saying, I have sinned in that I have betrayed the innocent blood. And they said, What is that to us? see thou to that. 5 And he cast down the pieces of silver in the temple, and departed, and went and hanged himself.

6 And the chief priests took the silver pieces, and said, It is not lawful for to put them into the treasury, because it is the price of blood.

7 And they took counsel, and bought with them the potter's field, to bury strangers in. 8 Wherefore that field was called, The field of blood, unto this day.

9 Then was fulfilled that which was spoken by Jeremiah the prophet, saying, And they took the thirty pieces of silver, the price of him that was valued, whom they of the children of Israel did value; 10 And gave them for the potter's field, as the Lord appointed me.

Jesus is tried before the governor who marvels that He neither defends Himself nor refutes the charges made against Him. All of this must happen in order to fulfill Scripture. Verses 11-18:

11 **And Jesus stood before the governor: and the governor asked him, saying, Art thou the King of the Jews? And Jesus said unto him, Thou sayest.**

12 **And when he was accused of the chief priests and elders, he answered nothing.** 13 **Then said Pilate unto him, Hearest thou not how many things they witness against thee?** 14 **And he answered him to never a word; insomuch that the governor marvelled greatly.**

15 **Now at that feast the governor was wont [accustomed] to release unto the people a prisoner, whom they would [choose].** 16 **And they had then a notable prisoner, called Barabbas.**

17 **Therefore when they were gathered together, Pilate said unto them, Whom will ye that I release unto you? Barabbas, or Jesus which is called Christ?** 18 **For he knew that for envy they had de-**

livered him.

When the governor sat down on the judgment seat to render his decision, he received a note from his wife. Verses 19-25:

19 When he was set down on the judgment seat, his wife sent unto him, saying, Have thou nothing to do with that just man: for I have suffered many things this day in a dream because of him. 20 But the chief priests and elders persuaded the multitude that they should ask [for] Barabbas, and destroy Jesus.

21 The governor answered and said unto them, Whether of the twain [two] will ye that I release unto you? They said, Barabbas. 22 Pilate saith unto them, What shall I do then with Jesus which is called Christ? They all say unto him, Let him be crucified.

23 And the governor said, Why, what evil hath he done? But they cried out the more, saying, Let him be crucified.

24 When Pilate saw that he could pre-

vail nothing, but that rather a tumult was made, he took water, and washed his hands before the multitude, saying, <u>I am innocent of the blood of this just person</u>: see ye to it.

<u>25 Then answered all the people, and said, His blood be on us, and on our children.</u>

Notice the last verse. Matthew records that all the people said, "His blood be on us, and on our children!"

Their choice was made. Pilate freed Barsabbas and Jesus began His suffering. Verses 26-28:.

26 Then released he Barabbas unto them: and when he had scourged Jesus, he delivered him to be crucified.

27 Then the soldiers of the governor took Jesus into the common hall, and gathered unto [around] him the whole band of soldiers. 28 And they stripped him, and put on him a scarlet robe.

They began to mock and ridicule Him while calling Him the King of the Jews. Verses 29-33:

29 And when they had platted [made] a crown of thorns, they put it upon his head, and a reed in his right hand: and they bowed the knee before him, and mocked him, saying, <u>Hail, King of the Jews!</u> 30 And they spit upon him, and took the reed, and smote him on the head.

31 And after that they had mocked him, they took the robe off from him, and put his own raiment on him, and led him away to crucify him.

32 And as they came out, they found a man of Cyrene, Simon by name: him they compelled to bear his cross. 33 And when they were come unto a place called Golgotha, that is to say, a place of a skull,

All of this began in the Garden of Gethsemane that morning. In just one morning, He was arrested, charged, arraigned, summarily judged, and sentenced. All this, in spite of the fact that He was without guilt as determined by the presiding judge. However, the religious leaders had the crowd demand His death. The people chose Barsabbas to be freed while leaving Jesus to be sentenced to death.

Jesus was offered a concoction mixed with gall. After tasting it, He refused to take it. I believe it was a form of toxin to reduce the pain He would suffer. Jesus chose to experience the unmitigated pain of the crucifixion. Verses 34-37:

> 34 **They gave him vinegar to drink mingled with gall: and when he had tasted thereof, he would not drink.**

> 35 **And they crucified him, and parted his garments, casting lots: that it might be fulfilled which was spoken by the prophet, They parted my garments among them, and upon my vesture did they cast lots. 36 And sitting down they watched him there;**

> 37 **And set up over his head his accusation written, <u>THIS IS JESUS THE KING OF THE JEWS</u>.**

This inscription was determined by the Governor based upon his understanding of the facts. It was by divine intervention that allowed the charge against Him to become His title published for all the world to see. From the Gospel of Luke, we learn that this superscription was written in three languages: Greek, Latin, and Hebrew. (See Luke 23:38).

Jesus hung on the Cross between two men who were convicted thieves. Crucifixion was a brutal display of the justice and power of Rome. It was intended as a deterrent to others. Verses 38-43:

38 **Then were there two thieves crucified with him, one on the right hand, and another on the left.**

39 **And they that passed by reviled him, wagging their heads, 40 And saying, Thou that destroyest the temple, and buildest it in three days, save thyself. If thou be the Son of God, come down from the cross.**

41 **Likewise also the chief priests mocking him, with the scribes and elders, said, 42 He saved others; himself he cannot save. If he be the King of Israel, let him now come down from the cross, and we will believe him.**

43 **He trusted in God; let him deliver him now, if he will have him: for he said, I am the Son of God.**

The two thieves between whom the Savior hung spoke through their pain with gritted teeth.. Their words are poignant in their effect. Verse 44:

44 The thieves also, which were crucified with him, cast the same in his teeth.

From the text, we know it was about noontime as the Jews begin the measurement of both their day and evening at six o'clock. Verses 45-46:

45 Now from the sixth hour there was darkness over all the land unto the ninth hour.

46 And about the ninth hour Jesus cried with a loud voice, saying, Eli, Eli, lama sabachthani? that is to say, My God, my God, why hast thou forsaken me?

Jesus Christ took upon Himself the sin of the world. Righteous in all His actions, the perfect Lamb of God became the Sin. His Father withdrew from this collective Sin and Jesus felt His withdrawal.

The crowd which stood about Him heard His words. Verses 47-48:

47 Some of them that stood there, when they heard that, said, This man calleth for Elias.

48 And straightway one of them ran, and took a spunge, and filled it with vinegar, and put it on a reed, and gave him to drink. 49 The rest said, Let be, let us see whether Elias will come to save him.

The bystanders, mostly Jews, wanted Him to be left alone so that they could see if Elijah would come to save Him. Verses 50-53:

50 Jesus, when he had cried again with a loud voice, yielded up the ghost.

51 And, behold, the veil of the temple was rent in twain from the top to the bottom; and the earth did quake, and the rocks rent;

52 And the graves were opened; and many bodies of the saints which slept arose, 53 And came out of the graves after his resurrection, and went into the holy city, and appeared unto many.

So profound were these happenings that their effect even caused the Roman centurion in charge to remark. Verse 54:

54 Now when the centurion, and they

that were with him, watching Jesus, saw the earthquake, and those things that were done, they feared greatly, saying, Truly this was the Son of God.

It was extremely difficult for those who were His followers to watch and, therefore, many watched from a distance. Verses 55-56:

> 55 And many women were there beholding afar off, which followed Jesus from Galilee, ministering unto him: 56 Among which was Mary Magdalene, and Mary the mother of James and Joses, and the mother of Zebedee's children.

One of His followers, a wealthy man, went to Pilate and pleaded for His body. Verses 57-60:

> 57 When the even [evening] was come, there came a rich man of Arimathaea, named Joseph, who also himself was Jesus' disciple: 58 He went to Pilate, and begged [for] the body of Jesus. Then Pilate commanded the body to be delivered.

> 59 And when Joseph had taken the body,

**he wrapped it in a clean linen cloth, 60
And laid it in his own new tomb, which
he had hewn out in the rock: and he
rolled a great stone to the door of the
sepulchre, and departed.**

The women followed at a distance huddled together
in their sorrow. Verses 61:

**61 And there was Mary Magdalene, and
the other Mary, sitting over against the
sepulchre.**

The anguish of the disciples who shared his
earthly ministry for three years and the other followers were overwhelmed with grief. Like all the days
before it, the sun came up the next morning. The religious leaders sought to manage the situation and
went to Pilate concerning the body. Verses 62-66:

**62 Now the next day, that followed the
day of the preparation, the chief priests
and Pharisees came together unto Pilate, 63 Saying, Sir, we remember that
that deceiver said, while he was yet
alive, After three days I will rise again.**

**64 Command therefore that the sepul-
chre be made sure until the third day,**

lest his disciples come by night, and steal him away, and say unto the people, He is risen from the dead: so the last error shall be worse than the first.

65 Pilate said unto them, Ye have a watch: go your way, make it as sure as ye can.

66 So they went, and made the sepulchre sure, [secure by] sealing the stone, and setting a watch.

32

Matthew 28

The sacrifice of the Passover Lamb took place on the day of Passover. The day that followed was the Sabbath and God's day of rest. After the Sabbath, God did a mighty work. He resurrected His Son from the dead. About six that morning, women came to attend to His body. Matthew 28:1-3:

> 1 **In the end of the sabbath, as it began to dawn toward the first day of the week, came Mary Magdalene and the other Mary to see the sepulchre.**
>
> 2 **And, behold, there was a great earthquake: for the angel of the Lord descended from heaven, and came and rolled back the stone from the door, and sat upon it.** 3 **His countenance was like lightning, and his raiment white as**

snow:

Pilate had commanded that Roman soldiers be place at the entrance to the tomb to guard against theft of Jesus' body. They are referred to as "the keepers." Verses 4-5:

> 4 **And for fear of him [the angel] the keepers did shake, and became as dead men. 5 And the angel answered and said unto the women, Fear not ye: for I know that ye seek Jesus, which was crucified.**

To these women who came to tend to His body, the angel makes a bewildering statement. They are the first to receive the news that their Savior has risen. Verses 6-7:

> 6 **He is not here: for he is risen, as he said. Come, see the place where the Lord lay. 7 And go quickly, and tell his disciples that he is risen from the dead; and, behold, he goeth before [ahead of] you into Galilee; there shall ye see him: lo, I have told you.**

Such news! How could they contain themselves! They immediately left to bring this good news to the others. Verse 8:

8 And they departed quickly from the sepulchre with fear and great joy; and did run to bring his disciples word.

The women were filled with joy and questions as they went their way. Jesus met them face to face. Comforted by His presence, they fell at His feet worshipping Him. Verse 9:

9 And as they went to tell his disciples, behold, Jesus met them, saying, All hail. And they came and held him by the feet, and worshipped him.

With words of assurance, He sends them on their way. Verse 10:

10 Then said Jesus unto them, Be not afraid: go tell my brethren that they go into Galilee, and there shall they see me.

After the Roman guards recovered from their fright, they found the angel gone and the tomb empty. They immediate went to report this to the authorities. Verses 11-15:

11 Now when they were going, behold, some of the watch came into the city, and shewed unto the chief priests all the things that were done.

12 And when they were assembled with the elders, and had taken counsel, they gave large [sums of] money unto the soldiers,

13 Saying, Say ye, His disciples came by night, and stole him away while we slept. 14 And if this come to the governor's ears, we will persuade him, and secure you. 15 So they took the money, and did as they were taught [told]: and this saying is commonly reported among the Jews until this day.

The women brought the message to the disciples as the angel had instructed them. They were to meet Jesus in Galilee. Verses 16-17:

16 Then the eleven disciples went away into Galilee, into a mountain where Jesus had appointed them. 17 And when they saw him, they worshipped him: but some doubted.

As we arrive at the end of the Gospel of Matthew, we have come a long way. We learned about

His geneaology and how He fulfilled all the prophecies that concerned Him. Matthew recorded Jesus' life and ministry on earth ending with His historic death, burial, and resurrection. He finishes with Jesus' words that must be understood within their intended context. Verse 18:

> 18 **And Jesus came and spake unto them, saying, All power is given unto me in heaven and in earth.**

The verses that follow are perhaps the most misunderstood and misinterpreted verses in the New Testament. We saw that Jesus came to fulfill the promises made to the fathers: Abraham, Isaac, and Jacob. Paul, the Apostle to the Gentiles, confirms this in Romans 15:8:

> 8 **Now I say that <u>Jesus Christ was a minister of the circumcision for the truth of God, to confirm the promises made unto the fathers</u>:**

We also know that Jesus sent the Twelve to the children of Abraham. Matthew 10:5-6:

> 5 **<u>These twelve Jesus sent forth</u>, and commanded them, saying, <u>Go not into the way of the Gentiles, and into any</u>**

city of the Samaritans enter ye not: 6 But go rather to the lost sheep of the house of Israel.

And, as they went their way, what would be the message they would bring? Verse 7:

7 And as ye go, preach, saying, The kingdom of heaven is at hand.

They are to bring the Gospel of the Kingdom promised to King David. Furthermore, they are to bring this gospel to the "lost sheep of Israel."

With that said, we can understand the context of the closing words. The preaching of the Gospel of the Kingdom will remain the same "even unto the end of the world" (v. 20). Matthew 28:19-20:

19 Go ye therefore, and teach all nations, baptizing them in the name of the Father, and of the Son, and of the Holy Ghost:

20 Teaching them to observe all things whatsoever I have commanded you: and, lo, I am with you alway, even unto the end of the world. Amen.

Epilogue

The Gospel of Matthew must be seen as a continuation of the Old Testament. Nothing had
changed! Israel was still under the Mosaic Covenant
and the Law. God made a promise to King David
that His kingdom would be eternal and ruled over
by his Son. The Gospel of Matthew begins with the
geneaology of Christ. Matthew establishes that Jesus
is the Son of David and the legitimate heir to his
throne.

We examined the prophecy received by the
Prophet Daniel. It concerned the fulfillment of this
Kingdom promise and laid out a timeline for us. Of
the 490 years spoken of in this prophecy, 483 years
were completed at the point when the Messiah was
"cut off." This means only seven years remain. However, something happened. God did not change His
mind. His promises and prophecies to Israel remain
unchanged. However, these seven remaining years
were temporarily suspended. To understand the
cause and make a judgment concerning the truth, we

must first consider all the evidence for ourselves in order to make an informed decision.

I go into great detail concerning this in *The Glorious Destiny of Israel: The Fulfillment of God's Promises and Prophecies To Israel.* For those looking for answers and explanations, this book presents the biblical evidence you need to consider. The book remains dedicated to presenting the Gospel of the Kingdom for the children of Abraham. I faced opposition from fellow Christians who were upset that I did not try to convert Jews to the Gospel of Grace. However, my job, as I see it, is to explain the Word of Truth rightly-divided. Each reader should make their own decision based upon the evidence!

There is one chapter in the Gospel of Matthew where Jesus specifically deals with the end times and the establishment of the eternal Kingdom. Matthew 24:13-15:

> 13 **But he that shall endure unto the end, the same shall be saved.** 14 **And this gospel of the kingdom shall be preached in all the world for a witness unto all nations; and then shall the end come.**
>
> 15 **When ye therefore shall see the abomination of desolation, spoken of by**

Daniel the prophet, stand in the holy place, (whoso readeth, let him understand:)

Is this not the goal of all students of God's Word: to read and understand His Word?

These remaining seven years are currently being held in abeyance. The rulers of Israel rejected the Messiah. Now, God is presently dealing with the Gentiles. It starts in the Book of Acts. (See Acts 28:28.) The Age of Grace begins with the conversion of the Apostle Paul and ends with the Rapture. When this happens, the Age of Grace will end and the seven remaining years of Daniel's prophecy will begin. Those interested in the details of the Gospel of Grace and God's offer through the Apostle Paul should read *Letters To Theophilus: Are You Ready For The End Times?*

For those who follow the Gospel of Grace, you should know that the Gospel of Matthew was *not* written *to* you. It was written *for* you. From it, you can understand Israel's role in God's restoration of His Creation and God's exclusive offer to the children of Abraham. Paul warns Grace Believers not to mix these two gospels. (See Galatians 1:6-9.) To do so will destroy your gospel's message. There is no requirement for works under the Gospel of Grace.

However, the Gospel of the Kingdom does have a requirement of works. They must believe that Jesus is the Messiah and the Son of God. They must repent from their sins and return to God and follow the intent of the Law not the letter of the Law. Finally, they must continually prove their faith by good works.

Look at Jesus' instructions to the disciples in Matthew 28:20:

> 20 **Teaching them to observe [do] all things whatsoever I have commanded you . . .**

Jesus did not come to abolish the Law but to fulfill it. He came to save the lost sheep of Israel who were under the Law. They were under the Law then and they remain under the Law to this day. Jesus instructed the Eleven to teach them to observe, do, obey or keep the Law. For three years, Jesus taught them to keep the Law. Again, they were to keep the intent of the Law; not the letter of the Law. They must also "endure unto the end" (Matt. 24:13). Then, Messiah will forgive them their sins at His Coming.

Jesus was asked by a Pharisee, "Master, which is the great commandment in the law?" (Matt 22:36). His answer to this question provides the means by which all the Law may be kept. Matthew 22:37-40:

276

37 Jesus said unto him, <u>Thou shalt love the Lord thy God with all thy heart, and with all thy soul, and with all thy mind.</u>

38 This is the first and great commandment. 39 And the second is like unto it, <u>Thou shalt love thy neighbour as thyself.</u>

40 <u>On these two commandments hang all the law and the prophets.</u>

Other GraceWord Publications

In English:

1st Corinthians: Dispensationally Considered
1st & 2nd Thessalonians: Dispensationally Con.
1st & 2nd Timothy & Titus: Dispensationally Con.
2nd Corinthians: Dispensationally Considered
Acts: Dispensationally Considered
Colossians & Philemon: Dispensationally Con.
Ephesians: Dispensationally Considered
Galatians: Dispensationally Considered
Hebrews: Dispensationally Considered
How Am I Wired?
Letters To Theophilus
Philippians: Dispensationally Considered
Romans: Dispensationally Considered
The Glorious Destiny Of Israel
The Gospel of John: Dispensationally Con.
The Gospel of Luke: Dispensationally Con.
The Gospel of Mark: Dispensationally Con.
The Hidden Gospel

The Seven Hebrew Epistles: Dispensationally Con.
Two Distinct Gospel Messages Of The New Test.

En español:

Cartas A Teófilo
Efesios: Dispensacionalmente considerado
El evangelio Oculto: Una vez fue un misterio . . .

About The Author

Dr. David Alan Greene has over thirty-five years of experience as an insurance agent selling both property and casualty as well as life insurance. During his career, he taught and explained the content and meaning of policies to his clients. Now retired, he devotes much of his time to teaching the Bible.

He obtained his Bachelor of Theology, Master of Biblical Studies, and Ph.D. in Biblical Studies from Evangelical Theological Seminary where he holds the position of Dean of Graduate Studies. He also holds a Ph.D. in Christian Counseling. He has written numerous biblical commentaries and books on rightly dividing the Word of Truth.

www.ingramcontent.com/pod-product-compliance
Lightning Source LLC
Chambersburg PA
CBHW071712120626

46550CB00001B/199